P9-CAL-752

THE CONTENTIOUS COMMUNITY

THE CONTENTIOUS COMMUNITY

Constructive Conflict in the Church

by
John M. Miller

THE WESTMINSTER PRESS
Philadelphia

COPYRIGHT ©1978 THE WESTMINSTER PRESS

All rights reserved—no part of this book may be repro-
duced in any form without permission in writing from
the publisher, except by a reviewer who wishes to quote
brief passages in connection with a review in magazine
or newspaper.

Scripture quotations from the Revised Standard Version
of the Bible are copyrighted 1946, 1952, © 1971, 1973
by the Division of Christian Education of the National
Council of the Churches of Christ in the U.S.A., and are
used by permission.

Book Design by Dorothy Alden Smith

First edition

Published by The Westminster Press ®
Philadelphia, Pennsylvania

PRINTED IN THE UNITED STATES OF AMERICA

9 8 7 6 5 4 3 2 1

Library of Congress Cataloging in Publication Data

Miller, John Michael, 1939–
    The contentious community.

    1. Church controversies. I. Title.
BV652.9.M54   273   78–3682
ISBN 0–664–24198–0

To
my wife,
my parents,
and
Elam Davies,
all of whom have been
my most valued advisers
for the ministry

Contents

Preface

Has anyone ever asked you, his voice laced with incredulity, why on earth you are associated with the church? The implication always seems to be that the church is so flawed, so imperfect, so contentious in its behavior, that any right-thinking person should avoid it at all costs. Otherwise, it is alleged that your purported moral judgement and ability to make objective assessments are severely jeopardized. Quite simply, the question is asked about the church, "What's a nice person like you doing in a place like this?"

This little book is an attempt to answer that question. First it explores the sometimes bellicose nature of the church, and then it seeks to put in a good word for the church and its contentious community, flaws and everything else. Not all our squabbles in the church are badges of honor, but they're not all smudges on our character either. Sometimes the church must contend within itself in order to move forward and progress.

Besides, I'd rather be part of a contentious community that is redeemed than a supposedly unsullied secular society that doesn't—and I trust this is accurate—have a *prayer*. It is clear that church people are not better than people outside the church, and in fact at times we have a quite remarkable ability to make ourselves appear worse. But we believe that we are God's people and that he accepts us as his people.

Therefore it is a great credit to God that he does not seem to mind being stuck with us. Comforting, that, especially when we feel misgivings about our contentiousness.

There are many individuals in particular and droves of folks in general whom I wish to thank for their influence in making me feel a part of Christ's church. As I calculate it, there are a dozen congregations with which I have had a direct association in both my youth and my adulthood, and I am grateful to them all for putting up with me. The congregations and church staffs of the three churches I have served as an ordained minister especially have convinced me that the church is the only place to be, even when there was something less that unanimity among the Christians over what the church is or is supposed to be doing.

Let us therefore turn to our brief discussion of the nature of that wonderfully yeasty and feisty fellowship, the Church of Jesus Christ.

J.M.M.

Morristown, New Jersey
February, 1978

The Nature
of the Warfare

Almost twenty centuries ago a Galilean carpenter-turned-rabbi was traveling throughout the towns and villages of Galilee and Judea, preaching the astounding Good News of the kingdom of God. With him were twelve men whom he had carefully selected. Before his sojourn with them was finished, Jesus of Nazareth discovered that:

1. Peter, the natural leader, did not always lead.

2. Matthew, the tax collector, presented a bad public relations problem. And some of the other disciples didn't help a whole lot either. The smell of fish, after all, attracts more cats than catechumens.

3. Rivalry among the Twelve threatened to destroy their relationship, as when James and John tried to guarantee positions of honor for themselves in the kingdom of heaven. The others allowed as how the two brothers had more nerve than brass monkeys to suggest such a thing. Besides, they deserved as much consideration for the top spots as James and John. Maybe more, since in their natural humility the thought to attempt to arrange such prominence would never have entered their minds.

4. Judas, perhaps the most intellectually gifted of the Twelve, felt betrayed by Jesus, and thus felt the need to betray him back. However, the Pharisees didn't require his services; they would have accomplished their purposes with-

out Judas or their thirty soiled pieces of silver.

5. In the end, when he needed their presence most, Jesus experienced only the glaring absence of his disciples. He faced the agony of his trial and scourging alone. The Galilee giants were midgets in the clutch.

History is kind to those who are fortunate enough to be on a winning team once the victory is assured. Thus it is that we look back on the disciples with rather more fondness and admiration than was their due before Easter made certain the conquest of Christ. If they were special, it was because the power of Christ within them made them special. Left to themselves, they would have been just that: left to themselves. But Jesus knew he could change them. And change them he did.

The first two generations of Christians are one of the most remarkable collections of people assembled at one time and in one place that the world has ever known. Within twenty-five years of the resurrection they had revolutionized Judea. Within seventy-five years they had prepared the foundation for a new social structure that was to revolutionize the Roman Empire. And a little more than two centuries beyond that, the emperor himself, Constantine, was to espouse Christianity. A truly remarkable group, these early Christians. But we are getting a little ahead of the story.

Probably most of us do not give much thought to what it must have been like in the first century of the church's existence. If we do think about it, we imagine that everyone was yoked together in the fellowship of Christian love, striving as one to advance the kingdom, united by evangelical zeal to go out into the world, preaching and baptizing in the name of Christ. Nose to the grindstone, shoulder to the wheel! Onward, Christian soldiers, marching as to war!

Marching as to war, yes; yoked together, striving as one, united, no. The first Christians had the same sort of ecclesiastical brouhahas as we have. There were far fewer of these squabbles, to be sure, because there were far fewer Christians. But the percentages were likely the same. Some of those church leaders of the first century were as anxious to be on the same team as would be, say, the Duke of Wellington and Napoleon Bonaparte, or Winston Churchill and Adolf Hitler.

If we are ever going to understand the true nature of the growth and development of Christianity, we must remove the rose-tinted spectacles we perpetually perch upon our proboscises whenever we look back on those original heroes of the faith.

Sometimes they were heroic, but frequently they looked and acted very much as we look and act.

Take Peter, for example. Admirable fellow, right? In the main, that's true. But I remember something about Peter starting to sink out on the waves of Galilee, when he came to the swift conclusion that walking on water was not such a snap after all. I recall that immediately after he declared that Jesus was the Messiah (the first person in all of history to do that), Peter contradicted Jesus, and Jesus told him, "Get behind me, Satan!" And I also recollect that on the most awful of nights Peter had gushed to Jesus, "Lord, I will never fail you," and within a few hours of that marvelous confession of comradeship, three times Peter said, "Jesus of Nazareth? Never heard of him."

Or take Mark. Not one of the better-known New Testament types, but he gets mentioned in Acts every now and again, and he managed to get a gospel into the New Testament when they had plenty of others from which to choose. Furthermore, 1.62 percent of all male children born in Keokuk, Iowa, are named Mark; 6 percent if you count middle names. But Paul thought so little of Mark that he wouldn't let him come along on one of his missionary journeys, even as a traveling unpaid bellhop.

Or there is Paul himself. Saul of Tarsus is *the* Christian without whom probably none of us would be a Christian. But, however much you might like to cast him in the light of a golden halo, he was a most difficult human being. Assuming that Jesus is in a class by himself, I would say that Paul had the greatest mind of anyone mentioned in the Bible. He was absolutely brilliant. But would you want him for your son-in-law, or your pastor? If he were your son or brother or father, you'd probably have some sort of complex. If he were your husband, it could only mean you were as ornery as he was, and you would both deserve each other. Great head, Paul; incredibly abrasive personality. George Bernard Shaw absolutely hated him. I think it was because Paul reminded him of himself. (I wonder whether that says more about Paul or George Bernard Shaw?)

How, you might ask, did Peter and Mark and Paul and all the rest really get along with one another? It's a question well worth asking. Read the lines of the New Testament, and it sounds like they were as unified a group as the church has ever known. Read between the lines, and you get another picture.

Look at Acts 15, for instance. Acts 15 tells about the first ecumenical council of the church.

The situation was this: Peter and Paul and the others had been out preaching the gospel everywhere they were welcomed, and in quite a collection of places where they weren't welcomed. An extremely crucial question had arisen. Should Christianity be preached only to Jews, or should it be proclaimed among the Gentiles as well? They decided it was universal, that everyone should hear the Good News.

But another question followed. Since Jesus was the Messiah of the Jews, and since all of the earliest Christians were Jews, shouldn't Gentiles first become Jews in order to become Christians? In other words, shouldn't they have to follow all of the Old Testament laws, and become orthodox Jews, if they wanted to be orthodox Christians?

Two answers were given to that question, which were, "I hope to tell you," and, "Not on your life." We are told in Acts 15:2 that when Paul and Barnabas heard some of the Christians were insisting that Gentile converts to Christianity must follow the Jewish religious law, they "had no small dissension and debate with them." Since we know Paul as we do elsewhere in the pages of the New Testament, that probably is putting it mildly. My guess is that the first ecumenical council was an ecclesiastical free-for-all of the highest and most vociferous character. When they met in Jerusalem, the shouting could be heard all the way to Damascus.

It was, you see, a monumental debate. In reality what was at stake was whether Christianity was going to become simply a Jewish heresy. Most of the Jews rejected Jesus as the Messiah. Most of the Gentiles rejected the religion of the Jews. If Gentiles were going to have to be circumcised and accept the 613 religious laws of the Old Testament, then precious few Gentiles would ever become Christians, and the prospects were dwindling that many more Jews were going to come into the fold.

Do you know who won? You *know* who won. It was the little tentmaker from Tarsus, and the big fisherman, and Barnabas, and Silas, and James. They are the people we hear more about. The ones we don't hear any more about are the losers, referred to as the Judaizers. They are nameless nobodies who swiftly disappeared from the New Testament scene.

You read what Acts 15 says and it appears that a group of cool, rational men convened, had a friendly chat, and wove a velvet agreement. It didn't happen like that at all. It was bitter. It was brutal. It was theologically, psychologically, and ecclesiastically bloody. When it was over, the church was split. The losers faded into the sands of the Judean desert, while the winners went on to write a New Testament and transform an empire.

The church then, as the church now, experienced deep, painful, divisive schisms. Besides being the only medicine that can really cure the world of its ills, the gospel is also a flashing broadsword that maims and cuts and kills. "Woe to you, scribes and Pharisees, hypocrites!" Jesus shouted at his enemies. "O foolish Galatians!" Paul greeted his friends in the faith from Asia Minor. To the church at Pergamum, the writer of the Revelation says, "I know where you dwell; it is where Satan's throne is." Not nice talk.

We often create for ourselves a fantasy, we who are Christians. The fantasy is that the church of Jesus Christ should be a company of people among whom there are no divisions, no disagreements; only harmony and love. What we understand so rarely is that the church can have both harmony and love *while at the same time* having divisions and disagreements. Disagreement does not necessitate disharmony. Division need not spawn hatred. Contention can exist within community.

It is precisely because people love both the Lord of the church and the church that so much of our ecclesiastical warfare arises. If we didn't care that much, what difference would it make whether we followed the Old Testament law or not? Or had bishops or not? Or went on marches, or built buildings, or had clergy, or gave money, or sent out mission workers, or made pronouncements, or received members, or dismissed members, or made demands of members, or went to church or not? If you don't care, you don't get excited about anything. But if you care (and millions upon millions have cared, billions by now, some of them to the point of torture and death), then you go at it tooth and claw. You fight for what you believe in and you give it everything you have because if you don't, they will win! And who are they anyway but a herd of ill-informed nincompoops who don't know Jesus Christ from jelly beans and who if it were in their power to do so would bring the church crashing down into an irreparable heap by a week from next Saturday?

When it's like that, folks, you fight. And for two thousand years, less a few, it's been perceived like that.

Don't get me wrong. I'm not knocking the church. Quite the opposite. The Christian church is the only institution in the world to have survived as long as it has, with its essential character as unchanged as it is. No government can come within eighteen hundred years of it for basic stability. No other religions, even the older ones of Hinduism and Buddhism, have managed to captivate such diverse and divergent peoples as Christianity has, nor have they made or tried to make a truly universal appeal. The church is an incredible marvel. Nothing less than the spirit of Jesus Christ moving among ordinary people could create such an ultraextraordinary instrument for God.

But the church has also had two thousand years of warfare, and I mean a war within. It might be much more pleasant were it not so. But were that the case, it wouldn't be the church, but a pale copy in sycophantic sepia of what the real church of muscles and corpuscles is supposed to be.

Still, in the light of what Jesus taught about love and harmony and selflessness, it is necessary to ask why the church seems to be continually bombarded as a result of its own internecine battles. There are many factors that explain the warfare. Let us focus here on five of them.

ONE. In the church, people sometimes do battle with one another because they feel so strongly about certain things. The key word here is *feel*. Feelings and emotions often are much more powerful than thought or reason in ecclesiastical disputes. We might wish it were otherwise, but it is not.

Let us take an example. For the past several years a great controversy has been raging within the Anglican (i.e., Episcopalian) churches of the world. Most recently the controversy has centered on the Episcopal Church in the United States of America. The question was this: Shall there, or shall there not, be female clergy?

In the best of all possible worlds, people would sit down together in faith and good fellowship, and after a friendly and in all probability lengthy debate, a conclusion would be reached. This conclusion would be based on biblical doctrine, sound theology, and careful reason. There is only one problem here. This, as you no doubt have discovered by now, is not the best of all possible worlds.

As an outsider looking in on the for-the-moment acrimonious Episcopalians, it is my judgment that it is not reason but emotion which has made this such an explosive issue for many of our Episcopalian brothers and sisters. On a rational level the issue is important, without question. But it is not all-important. It is not the only issue, not a live-or-die issue, not an if-they-don't-decide-it-my-way-I'll-quit issue. Yet that is precisely what it has become for many Episcopalians.

Why? Because emotions intervene between people and their own minds. Because hearts supersede heads. "I'll be hornswoggled (or something more drastic, if there is such a thing) before I'll let any fuzzy-headed female drop a wafer onto my heretofore undefiled tongue!" "We'll show those antediluvian diehards that you can't halt progress, and that's that!" "There is an international Communist conspiracy to destroy the church by getting women into the priesthood!" "Unless women are accepted into the priesthood, it is inevitable that the church will disintegrate—and soon!"

Those and many statements like them are long on emotion and short on reason. Certainly the question of female clergy is intellectually a complicated one. Certainly the decision to approve the concept among the bishops and deputies was arrived at by a process that was basically mental and theological. But for many Episcopalians, the entire matter is still an emotional issue, a question of feeling.

Or let's look at another example. I recall being in a meeting of dedicated church people in which a particularly thorny question was being hotly debated. No one was being attacked personally, but the issue was being attacked from all sides. In the midst of the fray, and without warning, one of the men suddenly burst into tears. He leaped up from his chair and fled from the room.

Now, what caused that? A momentary breakdown? Immaturity? Faulty tear ducts?

I think it was none of those things. The man was a normal, strong, mature human being. But he felt so deeply about the question being discussed that his feelings simply got the better of him.

When that happens, we in the church, at least the American, westernized church, are left in thumb-twiddling befuddlement, wondering what on earth to do next. We are trained from birth to deal with thoughts, but emotions baffle us. And in the church, a significant proportion of our warfare is the result of feelings and emotions.

TWO. Another explanation for church battles is that with astonishing regularity we Christians encounter *legitimate differences* among ourselves. It is not a case of feelings running high; it happens whenever there are two or more valid positions which can be taken with respect to any one question.

Take the mundane business of church buildings. To build, or not to build; that is the question.

As far as building a new church is concerned, the answers range from Now to Never, with Sometime or Other somewhere in between. Advisability, feasibility, necessity, and financing are all matters that must be discussed, and there are bound to be valid differences regarding such choices.

If someone is going to be excommunicated, you would think it should be over some crucial theological doctrine, or maybe the result of a heinous crime or grave moral indiscretion, right? Well, the last two Presbyterians to be excommunicated that I know about were a husband and wife who were members of a Presbyterian church in a Midwestern city. And the tussle was not over theology or morality; it was over bricks and mortar.

It seems that that congregation had decided to tear down their church building and build a new one some distance from the downtown area. The old building was Romanesque in its architecture. To some people, most definitely including this particular couple, Romanesque architecture is man's greatest artistic offering to God. To others, Romanesque architecture may be described, as I once heard a certain church building described, as "neo-American Railroad Station."

The upshot of the whole fracas is that the Presbyterian congregation of whom we are speaking voted to tear down the old building and move to a new one. The husband-wife team were so disturbed by this decision, and apparently were so determined to reverse it, that the session (governing board) of the church finally excommunicated them, after several previous censures and rebukes.

The kingdom of God does not stand or fall on Romanesque architecture, nor is it severely threatened by the decision of one congregation to remain at a downtown location or move out to the suburbs. However, those kinds of issues are of considerable import to all of us at various points in our individual lives or in the life of our congregations. There is no one clear, correct answer which will erase for all time the differences we have. Decisions must be made, but inevitably there are some who will be unhappy with whatever decision is made. Legitimate differences foster warfare.

THREE. Even where there are no basic differences among Christians, there is a whole rainbow of *shades of color* among us regarding everything. Christians come in all sizes and shapes. This is as true of minds and spirits as it is of bodies. You find ebullient Christians and indolent Christians, optimistic and pessimistic Christians, ultraeager, excited, enthusiastic, incisive, cool-thinking, placid, cautious, somewhat skeptical, and downright stick-in-the-mud Christians.

Because of the shading of both personalities and attitudes with respect to issues, it is inevitable that conflicts arise. If we were all the same, it would be much more peaceful, and as a corollary, dull as dishwater. We have neither dullness nor peace, if peace means a uniformity in which there are no disagreements.

People who prize uniformity see Christian shading as at

best a nuisance and at worst a constant threat. I would say to such people, it is a given reality, and as such it may as well be accepted. I would say further to them, what's so desirable about uniformity? If the artist has only one color of paint on his pallet, he can't paint much of a picture, can he? God, the ultimate artist of us all, created a rainbow of colors for his canvas, the church.

FOUR. Emotions, differences of opinion, and shading of personalities and issues create conflict in the church. Add *misunderstanding* to the list.

Many misunderstandings are simply the result of language. What one word means to one person may mean something entirely different to someone else. In Hebrew there is a word *hesed*, which is generally translated into English as the word "loving-kindness." I don't know what an average English-speaking person would take loving-kindness to mean, but almost certainly it would never be understood as it was by the Old Testament Hebrews. To them it was used to express God's relationship with man, and it was pictorial. *Hesed* is a father with his child, a mother with her baby, a friend with a friend, a child with a pet. It is an unbreakable bond, an invigorating warmth, peaceful sanctuary, the blessed assurance of the everlasting presence of God; it is—*hesed*. What else can one say? However we understand it, we probably misunderstand it, because it is not a word but a paragraph, a chapter, a book, a library, the whole anthology of man's relationship with God from the beginning.

Or there is the word *almah*. This one Hebrew word can mean two things, either "virgin" or "young woman." Isaiah 7:14, a famous passage, says, "Behold, a(n) *almah* shall conceive and bear a son, and shall call his name Immanuel." Does that mean virgin, or does it mean young woman? To many people, it would make no difference, but to some it matters a great deal. If it means "virgin," these people would insist, then it can be a foretelling of the birth of Jesus, seven and a half centuries before the fact, and it can support the ancient Christian tradition of the virgin birth. I don't know which is correct. But I do know this: if some insist on "virgin" and others insist on "young woman," somebody misunderstands something.

Such misunderstandings are the stuff of classic conflicts. The Christological controversies of the early church were exactly that sort of thing. Christians went after one another hammer and tongs because of how they understood certain Greek words, and how they believed others misunderstood them.

But we in the church have the capacity to misunderstand more than just words. We can mistake actions as well.

The Protestant Reformation in Germany may have occurred at the time it did because the Roman Catholic Church misunderstood the intentions of one Martin Luther. Luther was about as much of a revolutionary as Calvin Coolidge. When he tacked his Ninety-five Theses to the door of the castle church in Wittenberg, all he hoped for was a scholarly debate. Had he known that it would lead to the greatest disruption within Christendom since the break with the Eastern Orthodox churches in 1054, he would have gone off to a monastery to become a monk. Come to think of it, he *was* a monk. Monks aren't revolutionaries. Parish priests, maybe; monks—never.

Anyway, the church did misunderstand Luther's intentions, and the obedient Luther was goaded into becoming the forceful Luther, and finally the stubborn Luther. The Reformation would have come sooner or later, but it wouldn't have come under Martin Luther, except for that one crucial misunderstanding.

FIVE. As though the previous four factors are not enough to stimulate ecclesiastical warfare, there is another, less excusable, source. It is unvarnished *human cussedness, sinful cantankerousness.* What cruel treachery we Christians visit upon one another!

Of course, Christians don't have an exclusive patent on a

mean spirit. Other human beings are equally capable of culpable behavior, maybe even more culpable. But we have deluded ourselves into believing that Christians are supposed to be less sinful than other people.

Well, it isn't so. *Perhaps* we commit fewer sins (a highly debatable hypothesis), but we certainly are no less sinful. The question of sinfulness is a multiple-choice type, for there are many kinds of sin. Everyone is sinful. The question of how we commit sins is an essay type of question, and gives opportunity for great latitude of expression and explanation. Therefore the myriad instances of cantankerous activities in the church should come as no surprise to any of us.

And yet it continues to surprise us. It shocks and angers and saddens and befuddles us. So often we have seen it, but each new example leaves us feeling bewildered and somehow betrayed.

One of the Lutheran denominations in the United States recently split. Virtually everything I heard or read about that schism before it happened seemed to indicate that one of the leaders of that denomination was most unbending, unforgiving, and dogmatic. No doubt there are other interpretations; I am only expressing the impression that the media conveyed.

After the break was finalized, the leader in question appeared to be more flexible and forgiving. That was good. But it also was late. Too many had already felt that they had been branded and burned, and for them there could be no return to the mother church. Sin had intervened, and the process became irreversible.

There are reasons enough why the church so frequently goes to battle with itself. Add sin to the picture, and it's a wonder we got past Acts, chapter one.

•   •   •

But we did. We had to. There is no substitute for the church, much as we sometimes might wish there were.

All of us have some pithy statements as part of the pedagogical baggage we acquired from school. One I shall always remember from a lecture in church history is attributed to Cyprian, a third-century bishop of Carthage. "He can no longer have God for his Father, who has not the church for his mother."

It is absolutely true. One can no longer have God for his Father, who has not the church for his mother. Apart from the church, broadly defined, there is no knowledge of God. If people say they know God or know about God and yet do not consider themselves a part of the church, they know what they know only because they are acquainted with someone, or have read something by someone, who belongs to Christ's church. To speak of a real Christianity apart from the church is like talking about real baseball apart from players and base lines and a ball field.

This church, this *qâhâl*, this *koinōnia*, this fellowship of believers-and-sinners, is the instrument God has chosen to establish his kingdom on earth and to prepare mankind for his eternal kingdom. If he weren't God and we didn't know better, we might think he made a poor choice, because the church is and has always been such a feisty fellowship. However, he *is* God, and he must know what he's doing.

Besides, even though the history of the church is a record of almost continuous quarrels, they have been *lovers'* quarrels. Often we fight for and with that which we most love, because we care so deeply about it.

I remember that great hymn about the church written by that old war-horse, Timothy Dwight. Here was a grandson of Jonathan Edwards, and Jonathan Edwards was no shrinking violet himself. Dwight began his ministry as a chaplain in the Revolutionary army. After the war he became pastor of a congregation in Connecticut, and later he was installed as president of Yale University. Timothy Dwight lived at the end of the Enlightenment, a period during which organized religion took more than its just share of intellectual lumps. Yet he was able fervently to write:

> I love Thy Kingdom, Lord,
>   The house of Thine abode,
> The Church our blest Redeemer saved
>   With His own precious blood.
>
> I love Thy Church, O God:
>   Her walls before Thee stand,
> Dear as the apple of Thine eye,
>   And graven on Thy hand.

Lovers' quarrels have always existed in the church. It is inevitable from the nature of the church itself that thus it was and ever shall be. But if there are going to be quarrels, best they be of the lover's variety. It makes the war within ever so much more tolerable. Sometimes it makes the war positively exhilarating, and we might even say edifying.

1:

The Ideal Church

vs.

The Real Church

One of the most obvious conflicts in the church, either the church as a worldwide fellowship or as a local congregation, is the battle between the idealist and the realist. Somebody said, "Mankind is divided into two groups: those who divide mankind into two groups, and those who don't."

Whether or not that is true, it does appear that with respect to the nature of things people generally do fall into two categories: idealists and realists. Now, of course, there are gradations within those categories, such as realistic idealists, or idealistic realists, or idealists who are borderline realists, or realists who, if the truth were known, are actually closet idealists. In general, though, everyone seems to lean one way or the other, however slight the lean.

The question may be posed in numerous ways. Does God intend for the church to be an ideal institution? *Can* the church become ideal? *Should* the church become ideal? Will the church change very much from its present state? Are the realities such that we are always going to be faced with the same kinds of problems that have confronted all the Christians who have gone before us? Every day in every way are we getting better and better? *Any* day in *any* way are we getting even a little bit better? Are we always going to have conflict in Christ's church?

It never once crossed anybody's mind seriously to ask the

question, Is the church ideal? History has no record of even one starry-eyed idealist who figured things were so ducky in the church that God had decided to declare his work upon earth completed, since perfection had been attained by his people, and he'd better quit quickly lest some benighted oaf slip backward and necessitate God's trying to get everything in line again. *Whether* we are ideal has never been debated, because it is obvious that we are not. Whether we *should be* ideal or should strive for the ideal is something else again.

Let me begin the discussion by making an emphatic statement that may jar all hardened realists; but I know you'll survive, because realists always do: *The church must have some idealism.* It is not just that it *may* have idealism; it *must*.

You can't read the Sermon on the Mount without coming to that conclusion. You can't read Christ's parables of the kingdom without coming to that conclusion. You can't think about the disciples without coming to that conclusion. Heavens to Murgatroyd, Jesus certainly couldn't have been a one-hundred-percent card-carrying realist to have selected a squad like that! Realistically they were a most unpromising first string. You wouldn't even put them in the game when your team was ahead 112–0 with only two minutes left to play, unless you were something of an idealist. If Christ was idealistic, so ought Christians to be.

Let me continue by making another emphatic statement that may jar all soft and mushy idealists; but I know you'll survive, because you can't keep a good idealist down: *The church also must have some realism.* What do we think people, including Christians, are anyway, the embodiment of impeccable moral perfection?

Since Adam we have been a most difficult species to work with, and Adam himself was not much to write home about, either. We must realize that when you're dealing with humanity, you're faced with a most troublesome species. The worst of it all is that man is the only species God has to work with, at least on this planet. None of the animals on earth seems to be capable of operating a church, ideal, real, or otherwise. Can you imagine a hippopotamus playing a sixty-rank organ, or a hooded cobra making a pastoral call on a family of mongooses? Well, neither can I.

Still this idealist/realist dichotomy persists, and not only between some people who call themselves idealists and some other people who call themselves realists. The conflict exists within each of us personally. In our heads we see a kingdom, a heavenly kingdom, the church of Jesus Christ as it is meant to be, and then on Sunday morning we go to church and we see quite another entity, an earthly kingdom, an *earthy* kingdom, and *oy vay,* what a shock! There is Samantha Siddle-thwaite all snuggled up beside her husband Algernon and I know for a fact she's having an affair with an Argentinian corned beef importer (what else would you import from Argentina?) and whom does she think she's kidding? And there is the ever-grinning H. Brockington Farnsworth at his usual front-and-center ushering post who inherited a huge envelope business from his grandfather and who dumps so much effluent into the river that the fish if there were any wouldn't be able to open their mouths because their lips would be glued shut. And that fellow whatever-his-name-is who obviously is a communist because I heard he participated in a Veterans Opposed to Vietnam rally and you know what sort of group *they* are. And old Arthur L. Snavely over there who on the other hand is a fascist because he told an always reliable source whom he voted for in the last election. And yonder is that saintly Mrs. Cranston all by herself again who is married to the most impossible man in the civilized world who has passed off the worst of everything in him to their son Mephistopheles, our paper boy. If he manages to get the paper to us at all, he sees to it that it was first run over by a semitrailer or marinated overnight in a combination of goose grease and linseed oil. Idealism has a tough row to hoe when it is confronted by the likes of that. And everyone can cite chapter and verse for the likes of that, one case after the other.

What a grand and glorious and dubious and duncely enigma is the Christian church! It does so much and does it so magnificently, and it accomplishes a miniscule speck of next to nothing. But that's no surprise to anyone when you think about the kind of people whom the church allows to be its members. The church bears the people of God to the presence of the Almighty on its wings of power and grace, and it drives them to the frontiers of distraction because it can't even move, let alone get off the ground.

Jesus had conflicts within himself on the basic issues of idealism and realism. Glancing swiftly at some of the verses from the Sermon on the Mount, for example, you come across the following statements from that paean of the ideal.

"For I tell you, unless your righteousness exceeds that of the scribes and Pharisees, you will never enter the kingdom of heaven." (Matt. 5:20.) That is stiff stuff, for most of the scribes and Pharisees were highly exemplary in their personal lives. The word "Pharisee" means "Puritan." And Jesus wants us to be purer than the Puritans?

"You have heard that it was said to the men of old, 'You shall not kill; and whoever kills shall be liable to judgment.' But I say to you that every one who is angry with his brother shall be liable to judgment; whoever insults his brother shall be liable to the council, and whoever says, 'You fool!' shall be liable to the hell of fire." (Matt. 5:21-22.) I don't know about you, but I find that quite a stinger. All the more so since Jesus is deadly serious.

"You have heard that it was said, 'You shall not commit adultery.' But I say to you that every one who looks at a woman lustfully has already committed adultery with her in his heart." (Matt. 5:27-28.) Surely in these liberated days the reverse of that must apply to women too! Let's get as many into this scalding caldron as we can. Perhaps it will cool down the water a bit.

"If your right eye causes you to sin, pluck it out and throw it away; it is better that you lose one of your members than that your whole body be thrown into hell." (Matt. 5:29.) If we take this at its face value, the entire human race will end up as blinded quadriplegics whose tongues also have been surgically excised.

"You have heard that it was said, 'An eye for an eye and a tooth for a tooth.' But I say to you, Do not resist one who is evil. But if any one strikes you on the right cheek, turn to him the other also." (Matt. 5:38–39.) A zinger.

"You have heard that it was said, 'You shall love your neighbor and hate your enemy.' But I say to you, Love your enemies and pray for those who persecute you." (Matt. 5: 43–44.) Owwwwww-eeeeeee!

And then, as though all these extraterrestrial demands were not enough, Jesus concludes, "You, therefore, must be perfect, as your heavenly Father is perfect" (Matt. 5:48). Thank heaven for Luke's version of this saying: "Be merciful, even as your Father is merciful" (Luke 6:36). That's idealistic, but at least it seems to be more in the manner of mortals.

Jesus was serious in his idealism. He really meant that his followers should stand head and shoulders above the rest of the crowd in moral integrity. Occasionally Jesus used hyperbole, as when he said in the Sermon on the Mount, "Why do you see the speck that is in your brother's eye, but do not notice the log that is in your own eye?" (Matt. 7:3). That is overstatement. It is meant as a joke. But while Jesus often joked, he never kidded, at least not when he was being serious, and in the Sermon on the Mount, he was being very serious.

Is such idealistic behavior possible? Some of Christ's followers have thought so. Tolstoy tried to pattern his whole life after the Sermon on the Mount. Gandhi, who accepted the Christian ethic if not the Christian faith, cast off a colonial yoke by means of the ethical ideals of Jesus.

On the other hand, Jesus was also clearly realistic. Consider a few sayings from some of the chapters immediately following the Sermon on the Mount. They are what Bismarck might have called *Realtheologie,* had he devoted himself to theology rather than politics.

When a would-be disciple asked if Jesus would wait for him until after he had seen to his father's burial, Jesus said, "Follow me, and leave the dead to bury their own dead" (Matt. 8:22). There's no point in saying you're going to become a Christian soon. Do it now, or you'll never do it. Stern realism.

Looking out over the disparate masses of people who trailed him wherever he went, Jesus said to his disciples, "The harvest is plentiful, but the laborers are few" (Matt. 9:37). How true it is! There are red, ripe apples to be picked everywhere, but nearly everyone is too shy, or feels lacking in the proper skills or experience for this arduous endeavor, or is just too pooped to pluck.

When he commissioned the twelve apostles, and sent them out, Jesus said, "Behold, I send you out as sheep in the midst of wolves; so be wise as serpents and innocent as doves" (Matt. 10:16). That's realism! Christian discipleship is a sneaky, straightforward affair; there's the circuitous truth of it.

"Beware of men; for they will deliver you up to councils, and flog you in their synagogues, and you will be dragged before governors and kings for my sake, to bear testimony before them and the Gentiles." (Matt. 10:17–18.) More of that hard realism. *If* you're going to be a Christian, a big If, you're going to get into trouble for it. You can no more avoid it than water can avoid being wet.

"When they persecute you in one town, flee to the next." (Matt. 10:23.) If you don't score points quickly, you'd better find another game. Otherwise you're just wasting your time —and God's.

But Jesus was not always so clearly either an idealist or a realist. Sometimes he vacillated back and forth in the midst of the same thought, practically the same sentence. Giving the apostles their marching orders, he said, "Go nowhere among the Gentiles, and enter no town of the Samaritans, but go rather to the lost sheep of the house of Israel" (Matt. 10:5–6). Obviously good, realistic advice. If Christians were going to make any headway at all at that early point in the gospel's story, it would be among Jews, because Jews shared the same rich heritage as Jesus and his disciples. But immediately after having been so realistic about the disciples' prospects, he became idealistic about the disciples themselves: "And preach as you go, saying, 'The kingdom of heaven is at hand.' Heal the sick, raise the dead, cleanse lepers, cast out demons. You received without pay, give without pay. Take no gold, nor silver, nor copper in your belts, no bag for your journey, nor two tunics, nor sandals, nor a staff; for the laborer deserves his food" (Matt. 10:7–10). That requires a leap of faith which leaves most of us well back from any danger of hurling ourselves over the unexplored edge.

If Christ himself felt ambivalent about idealism and realism, is it any wonder that Christians feel the same way? And is it surprising that that dichotomy produces conflict in the church?

The church must come closer to the ideal, but it isn't doing it! The church must get its head out of the clouds and its feet on the ground, but it isn't doing it! Why doesn't the church get with it? Why doesn't the church think the way *I* think!

The church is like a children's choir gathered in the sanctuary of God to sing praises to his name. Standing there in the chancel is the hope for a truly new generation, and the assurance that no one is well advised to hold his breath in the anticipation that there is going to be one. Innocence and guile are perched on the edge of the platform, waiting to burst forth in song or shove some unsuspecting freckle-faced being to an ignominious landing three feet below. And it isn't that Bonnie is innocent and Bobby is full of guile; it is that innocence and guile, the ideal and the real, are coursing through the veins of each. As St. Augustine sardonically

stated it more than fifteen hundred years ago, "The innocence of children may be more a matter of weakness of limb
than it is purity of heart."

The battle between idealists and realists has always been
accentuated by the factor of age. Young people tend toward
idealism, and older people toward realism. Without question
there are multitudinous exceptions to that rule, but it is generally true.

Nevertheless, either realism or idealism can slip into cynicism with respect to the other. Older people may look at
younger people, and instead of being realistic about them,
they sometimes become cynical. They don't say, "Oh, well,
I was young once, and I wasn't really much different from the
youth of today"; no, indeed. "A crowd of crazies; that's what
they are! Rock music and wild parties and rootless meander-
ings all over the face of the earth when they should be staying
in school and studying and working hard the way I did!" The
infection of cynicism sets in. And cynicism is as inimical to
realism as it is to idealism.

But it happens the same way on the other side. Some
young people weigh mankind and man's institutions on the
scales of idealism, and inevitably they are found wanting. As
a pastor I see it so frequently as it affects the church in
particular. The issue arises with the greatest predictability in
premarital counseling. More often than not I know the couple only casually, if at all, because one or the other or both
have been away from the community for the past several
years. During that time, or possibly before that time, they
had given up on the church. They have a vision of what the
church is supposed to be, and our congregation does not
come within ten light-years of their apocalypse. So they wash
their hands of the church—except for just now when they
want to be married within its momentarily-once-again sacred precincts.

I don't blame them for their disillusionment. The church
is disillusioning. It is far from ideal. They are absolutely cor-

rect; it isn't what it is supposed to be at all. But how, I ask myself, is it ever going to get better if the flower of its youth, the arsenal for its idealism, keeps disappearing from among its active membership? *Herr Gott im Himmel!* It's as though a college student in the latest sports car runs out of gas in the middle of the Mohave Desert. The heat is scorching, so he figures he'd better go for some gasoline or he may not survive. After he has walked down the blistering roadway for a couple of miles, an old man in a battered 1949 Chevrolet comes along and asks him if he wants a ride. "No, thanks," says the student. "That isn't my idea of a car you're driving." And he continues on in his lonely trek.

I attended a seminar once in which it was postulated that the individual should concentrate on his strengths, not on his weaknesses. In other words, give the best you possess, because your worst isn't worth giving. It may not even help that much to try to strengthen your weaknesses, since they may be as much of a "given" in you as blond hair or brown eyes.

What are you—an idealist? Give that to the church. God knows the church needs it. It is your best strength. It's your longest suit. Coupled with the suits of your partners, it may lead you to victory.

What are you—a realist? Give *that* to the church. God knows the church needs that too. It is your best strength, your longest suit, your contribution toward victory.

I love the parables of the kingdom. Jesus tells us that God's kingdom is yet to come; most of his parables have a future reference. And then he says to his disciples, and through them he says it to us, "The kingdom is among you." It is here! It is present! It has already happened! What a revolutionary, exciting, scary statement that is!

Which is the church going to be: idealistic or realistic, ideal or real? It is going to be both, because the church is above all *people,* and people come in both varieties, and both polarities are represented, however minutely, in every person.

Christ wants massive doses of idealism to be injected into the veins of his body, the church. He also wants massive doses of realism to be injected. He even can use surprisingly strong prescriptions of skepticism as well. You'd be amazed at the diseases the church can catch when it isn't properly inoculated.

Cynicism Christ won't tolerate at all; not at all! If cynicism is your long suit, forget it. Neither Christ nor his church needs it. Go peddle it someplace else. It has a street value of Zero. It has an ecclesiastical value of Minus Zero.

However, with all this idealism and realism and your occasional antibody of skepticism floating around, there is bound to be a reaction every now and then. Jesus never promised perfect health in his church. He just said we'd be a lot better off *in* the church than *out* of it.

It is a strange and wondrous mechanism, the body of Christ. Anyone who accepts everything about the church as it is and who thinks that it is realistic to assume that nothing is going to change has misjudged the power of Jesus Christ to transform humanity and human institutions. Anyone who believes idealistically that he is going to see a total transformation in the nature of the church in a short time or even in a lifetime has misjudged the restraining power of human nature.

What a prospect! What a battle! Can't we make it any clearer than that? Will these battles never cease?

2:

Hard-Core Christianity
vs.
Soft-Core Christianity

Is the church of Jesus Christ like a peach, or is it like a banana? Have you ever lain awake nights wondering about that? I can't understand why not.

Well, then, would you say the church is like a plum, or a strawberry? An avocado, or an orange? A date, or a fig? An olive, or a seedless grape?

The question is this: Is there an essential *something* about the church, a pit in the midst of the fruit, one living seed surrounded by a sweet but unessential goo, or is the church a total reality, seed *and* fruit, hard-core as well as soft-core?

Did you ever grab a cantaloupe at the grocery store when you were in a hurry? You had enough time to poke it on the top side, and found it firm, but when you got it home, you discovered that the bottom was spongy. Cantaloupe is a devious melon. Just when you think you have the perfect specimen, its mushy character will come through to fool you.

Some people feel that way about the church. It is all right when it is what it is supposed to be, which, in their opinion, is a hard-core organization of totally dedicated followers of Jesus Christ. But for them the problem is that hard-core church members are a distinct minority. The church, they say, is made up primarily of wishy-washy Christians. And a wishy-washy Christian, according to their definition, is no Christian at all. Thus the church is essentially an ecclesiastical fraud which soft-core would-be Christians are trying to perpetrate on the Lord of all life. And, they insist, he will not be defrauded.

They have plenty of support for their position. Consider these sayings of Jesus, for example:

The Case for Hard-Core Christianity

"Fear not, little flock, for it is your Father's good pleasure to give you the kingdom. Sell your possessions, and give alms; provide yourselves with purses that do not grow old, with a treasure in the heavens that does not fail, where no thief approaches and no moth destroys. For where your treasure is, there will your heart be also." (Luke 12:32–34.) Being a Christian is simple. Give up everything and you're there.

"Take heed then how you hear; for to him who has will more be given, and from him who has not, even what he thinks that he has will be taken away." (Luke 8:18.) If you don't give up everything, you will end up with less than nothing. A less than comforting thought.

"Every one to whom much is given, of him will much be required; and of him to whom men commit much they will demand the more." (Luke 12:48.) On the other hand, if you do give up everything, you'll be given everything. Except that everything will be expected of you. This is what is called a "slammed if you do and slammed if you don't" situation.

"For it is easier for a camel to go through the eye of a needle than for a rich man to enter the kingdom of God." (Luke 18:25.) Just in case anyone might think Jesus was talking about something else.

"Have faith in God. Truly, I say to you, whoever says to this mountain, 'Be taken up and cast into the sea,' and does not doubt in his heart, but believes that what he says will come to pass, it will be done for him. Therefore I tell you, whatever you ask in prayer, believe that you receive it, and you will."

(Mark 11:22–24.) Hard-core Christianity involves more than giving up things. It involves acquiring things, acquiring a dauntless faith. How many mountains did you move today? Or even semihummocks?

"No one who puts his hand to the plow and looks back is fit for the kingdom of God." (Luke 9:62.) Second thoughts are deadly. Well, on second thought. . . .

"Strive to enter by the narrow door; for many, I tell you, will seek to enter and will not be able." (Luke 13:24.) The hard core of Christianity is small. Many will desire to be there, but they aren't going to make it.

"Truly, I say to you, there is no one who has left house or brothers or sisters or mother or father or children or lands, for my sake and for the gospel, who will not receive a hundredfold now in this time, houses and brothers and sisters and mothers and children and lands, with persecutions, and in the age to come eternal life. But many that are first will be last, and the last first." (Mark 10:29–31.) In a way, this is encouraging. But then there is—

"If any one comes to me and does not hate his own father and mother and wife and children and brothers and sisters, yes, and even his own life, he cannot be my disciple." (Luke 14:26.) Taken at its face value, Christianity seems to be the greatest threat there is to that most basic of all social institutions, the family.

"Do you think that I have come to give peace on earth? No, I tell you, but rather division; for henceforth in one house there will be five divided, three against two and two against three; they will be divided, father against son and son against father, mother against daughter and daughter against her mother, mother-in-law against her daughter-in-law and daughter-in-law against her mother-in-law." (Luke 12:51–53.) Can anyone ever again sing, "Gentle Jesus, meek and mild"?

"If any man would come after me, let him deny himself and take up his cross and follow me. For whoever would save his life will lose it; and whoever loses his life for my sake and the gospel's will save it." (Mark 8:34–35.) The cross, the central symbol of Christianity, is a stern reminder of death. Jesus wants his people to shoulder a cross, not *his* cross, but *their own.* There is incredible tension in this invitation, friend. Jesus Christ is no pansy, and Christianity is no piece of cake.

"Whoever does not bear his own cross and come after me, cannot be my disciple." (Luke 14:27.) A German theologian was hanged by the Gestapo a few days before Germany capitulated at the end of World War II. Earlier, Dietrich Bonhoeffer had written, "When Christ calls a man, He bids him come and die." Hard-core Christianity cannot lightly be dismissed. It cannot be dismissed at all. It is *there.* It *exists.* Christ makes tremendous demands upon our lives. He demands everything.

• • •

And so,

"He who is not with me is against me, and he who does not gather with me scatters." (Luke 11:23.) It is very clear. Hard-core Christianity is the only kind of Christianity. A wishy-washy Christian is a contradiction in terms. Hard-core church members are the only kind of church members there are. Others who call themselves church members are self-deluded, pretend christians.

But then,

"For he that is not against us is for us." (Mark 9:40.)

Therein lies a dilemma. It is a question of Gospel purity; who is correct, Luke or Mark? Mark wrote his Gospel first. So is Luke wrong? Which did Jesus say? Or did he say both?

But it also is a question of the nature of the church. If only those who positively are one hundred percent *for* Christ are the real church, then by all means it is a hard-core institution. But if a Christian is simply someone who is not one hundred percent *against* Christ, then the church is a gigantic institution, encompassing not only Christmas and Easter Christians but people who have never signed their name on any church's dotted line, never attended church, wouldn't be caught dead attending church and who sometimes attend bodily only after they *are* dead, not to mention all those Hindus, Buddhists, Marxists, and Australian aborigines who may not be all that much *for* Jesus, but who certainly aren't *against* him.

Which brings us to

The Case for Soft-Core Christianity

"With men it is impossible, but not with God; for all things are possible with God." (Mark 10:27.) After having told his disciples that it was harder for a rich man to enter heaven than for a camel to go through the small door in the city gate (the needle's eye), Jesus turned right around and said that nevertheless the salvation of the apparently affluent is possible. (Citizens of Newport and Newport Beach: take heart; you may make it yet.)

"And blessed is he who takes no offense at me." (Matt. 11:6.) Here is still another indication that the stern Jesus of the previous passages holds out hope for those who exhibit less than total enthusiasm for the Christian mission.

"Come to me, all who labor and are heavy laden, and I will give you rest. Take my yoke upon you, and learn from me; for I am gentle and lowly in heart, and you will find rest for your souls. For my yoke is easy, and my burden is light." (Matt. 11:28–30.) Verily and in verity, this is the Credo of the Soft-Core. Never did gentler, kinder words fall on softer, squishier souls.

"Those who are well have no need of a physician, but those who are sick; I have not come to call the righteous, but sinners to repentance." (Luke 5:31–32.) Hard-core Christians would never claim sinlessness, but they generally don't boast of many mega-sins either, at least not recent ones. But here Jesus is telling us that it is sinners and only sinners, whether mega- or mini-sinners, whom he wants to bring into his church. Without question he wants to do something about sin once he gets them in, but sin is a necessary qualification before one is even handed an application blank. Perhaps those soft-core sinners on the fetid fringes of the church may not be totally beyond the pale after all.

"Woman, where are they? Has no one condemned you? Neither do I condemn you; go, and do not sin again." (John 8:10–11.) What an incredibly grace-filled Christ he is! Here is a woman who is guilty beyond any doubt of adultery, and Jesus tells her he does not condemn her! Might he also forgive us, soft-core followers that we are?

"But the tax collector, standing far off, would not even lift up his eyes to heaven, but beat his breast, saying, 'God, be merciful to me a sinner!' I tell you, this man went down to his house justified rather than the other; for every one who exalts himself will be humbled, but he who humbles himself will be exalted." (Luke 18:13–14.) There is Good News in the parables. To certain kinds of hard-core christians it is bad news because it opens the door to all kinds of soft-core Christians, but to other hard-core Christians it is Good News because it shows that God loves even soft-core christians and no-christians. God is love. He really is. It says so in the Bible.

" 'For this my son was dead, and is alive again; he was lost, and is found.' And they began to make merry." (Luke 15:24.) Those words go beyond every semblance of human logic. They are the manifesto of an unbelievably extravagant God. Anyone who ever doubted the validity of soft-core Christianity should read again the parable of the prodigal son. What a father is the father of that son! What a Father is the Father of us all!

Am I trying to give you the *soft* sell? Not on your peach pit, I'm not. Am I going for the *hard* sell? I'll be a banana if I do.

I'm trying to suggest that both are valid. Within the church of Jesus Christ there is a reality to both the hard-core and the soft-core. Jesus demands much of us and he demands little, we are going to have to do a great deal to be Christians, and *we* are not going to have to do one blessed thing, he will do it all for us.

We *must* limit the church only to the hard-core, and we *can't* limit the church only to the hard-core. Jesus is exclusive about who gets in, and Jesus is inclusive and wants everybody in. For these reasons the church has material for an endless lovers' quarrel.

Take baptism, for instance. Who should be baptized? If you're a Baptist, you would say that anyone who is old enough to believe in God and confess Jesus Christ as Lord and Savior and does believe and confess should be baptized. But if you're in one of the other churches, and numerically most of us are, the matter is not so clear-cut.

If a couple pop in off the street and ask a pastor to baptize their baby, should the pastor agree to do so? Should baptism be administered upon request for everyone who asks it? Should any questions be addressed to those parents regarding their own faith and their intention to bring up that child in the church, and not just deposit the child, like so many dollars in the bank, in the Sunday school every Sunday? Should the parents be members of a church themselves before the baptism of their child can take place? Should they be members of that particular church where they want their child baptized?

The elders of the Presbyterian Church in Morristown, New Jersey, have instituted a policy which says that at least one parent must be on the roll of our church before their child can be baptized. In the Presbyterian tradition, as in many traditions of other denominations, not to baptize a baby says nothing about the baby, but it does say something about the parents. All children are children of God anyway, and he is not going to hold anything against a child who has not been baptized. (This does not represent Roman Catholic doctrine, I readily admit.)

Is that policy a hard-core policy? I think not. On a scale of 1 to 10, 1 being "very soft" and 10 being "very hard," I would say that policy is 5½, maybe 6.

But believe me, sometimes I feel like a 10 on the basis of the reactions I get to it. To some parents it is incomprehensible that a church would not gladly welcome any baptism, even if the parents are not members of any church. And they may voice very strong objections. But where the shoe really pinches is with grandparents. If the grandparents are members of our church and the parents are not, and have no intention of being members of our congregation or any other, sometimes we really hear about it. I don't blame the grandparents for being upset, but I think their anger is misdirected. They should challenge their children, not the church. But such are the results of our hard-core/soft-core policy on baptism.

Who should be confirmed by the church? Only hard-core young Christians or soft-core ones too? And if soft, how soft? Has the church the right to insist that its young people attend worship regularly and attend confirmation classes? That does not seem unreasonable.

And yet if that policy is put into effect, it will mean that some youngsters will never be confirmed, because neither they nor their parents will see to it that they attend church or the classes on a regular basis. And if they go unconfirmed, some observers will probably say that they are lost to the church forever. Others will wonder whether the church ever had them in the first place. And a classic hard-core/soft-core blaze is kindled.

Or who should be married in the church, and for whom should a minister officiate at a wedding? Anybody? Everybody? Hard-core Christians only? If so, there would be fewer weddings these days than there already are. Soft-core Christians? People who may not be Christians at all, but who are respectable and nice despite that one deficiency?

Weddings are frequently the stickiest of wickets for the church's parsons and priests. If the clergy are going to get in Dutch, weddings are probably the prime candidates for putting them in the hollandaise sauce. I don't mean the wedding itself. That can get a parson in Dutch too, for everyone has an opinion about how a wedding should be organized, except grooms and fathers of grooms.

No, the fat first hits the ministerial fire over the question of whether there shall be a wedding, at least a *church* wedding, at all. What do you do when the bride and groom are not members of a church, do not believe in God or in Jesus Christ, want to write their own service—replete with readings from the Bhagavad-Gita, Lao-tzu, and Rod McKuen, have already chosen some of the finest secular music from the last half of the twentieth century, which in their opinion is the only period of fine music in all of human history—a year and a half ago set a date for the church for late July because it was the earliest open date at the place where the reception is to be held, and whose parents are such pillars of the church that should they even be jarred in the slightest the whole house of God will collapse and great will be the fall of it?

There is hard-core Christianity, and then again there is hard-core Christianity. Sometimes the pressures are rather on the stiff side, believe me. The minister asks, What does the church stand for? Does it stand for anything? Will it take a stand? Will *I* take a stand?

Then there are those times when despite your firmest resolves you break your own attempts at theological purity within the membership of Christ's church. I recall a wedding I performed in Chicago. Ours was a beautiful Gothic downtown church, and it was the dream of innumerable couples to have the bonds of matrimony knotted within our sacred confines. The answer was always No when there was no connection with our church or *the* church.

This was something else again, however. One day a well-dressed woman came in, followed by a very young couple. The mother asked, in firm tones that somehow lacked the usual inflection of a question, whether her daughter might be married, in our church, by me, that afternoon. There was not a chance in the world that I would accede to that request from total strangers so quickly—under normal circumstances.

The situation, I soon discovered, was this: the parents of the girl had driven to Ohio to fetch her and her boyfriend, who had been living there in what used to be called sin. However it might be described, it only took one glance at the daughter's figure to see that the primary question was which would occur first, matrimony or maternity. I judged her to be in her eleventh month. For this wedding to transpire in the usual order of things, it was now or never.

The girl and her beau were flower children of the '60s. I liked them immediately. I liked the mother, imposing countenance and all. I liked the father, when he appeared, and I gathered that he appeared only when he was programmed to appear.

After a conversation with the couple alone, I came to the conclusion that though they were too young to be married, and did not have much of a clue as to the nature of Christian marriage, and might well end up before long in a divorce court, nevertheless I wanted to do whatever I could to give them as good a beginning as possible on behalf of the church. It would legitimate the daughter's attempts to escape the powerful psychological clutches of her mother, who was a twentieth-century Lady Macbeth, with an equivalent amount of cunning and charm. It wasn't for the baby that I performed the wedding service. In some similar cases, I have advised others not to be married, at least not in the church, and to put the baby up for adoption. But for them I took the soft-core approach.

Charles Sheldon wrote one of the best-selling novels of all time around the question, "What would Jesus do?" *In His Steps* was the result.

What *would* Jesus do—now, here, in the twentieth century? There are so many complexities that we face in the church, and it is so hard to know whether we should take a hard or a soft approach to churchmanship.

What should we do about church rolls? Should inactive members be nursed along or pruned, given a shot in the arm or an ecclesiastical *coup de grace?* People suggest that the church should never remove anyone's name from its active roll, no matter how inactive that person might be, for someday that person may need the church, and its doors should always be open. Others say that such people need the church right now, despite their apparent lack of awareness of that need, but if they don't respond, the church is less than honest to retain their membership.

I know of a church whose governing board received new members every Sunday after the regular worship service. It was easier to join that church than it was to answer a three-question poll of the League of Women Voters—and it took less time. That church had the biggest roll of the softest-core members in Christendom.

Then there are denominations like the Mormons and Seventh-day Adventists and Nazarenes. There's no fooling around with those folks. A soft-core Nazarene has the consistency of a rock-hard Presbyterian. You can find ideologically hard-core Presbyterians, but you find them about as frequently as you run across nuns who have been named Playboy Bunny of the Year.

When officers of the United Presbyterian Church are ordained, whether as deacons, elders, or ministers, they are asked if they promise to pursue the "peace, unity, and purity" of the church. Most denominations probably have a similar vow. Hard-core Christians are long on purity, soft-core Christians are long on peace, and they fight like cats and dogs to achieve unity—on their own terms.

God must have a tussle within himself sometimes about what he expects us to be. He wants us to be spiritually as hard as nails, but he knows that emotionally and psychologically we're as soft as goose down.

One of my favorite Old Testament prophets is Hosea, who expresses God's own hard-core/soft-core dilemma so perfectly.

> When Israel was a child, I loved him,
>   and out of Egypt I called my son.
> The more I called them,
>   the more they went from me;
> they kept sacrificing to the Baals,
>   and burning incense to idols.
> . . . .
> My people are bent on turning away from me;
>   so they are appointed to the yoke,
>   and none shall remove it.
>
> How can I give you up, O Ephraim!
>   How can I hand you over, O Israel! . . .
> My heart recoils within me,
>   my compassion grows warm and tender.
> I will not execute my fierce anger,
>   I will not again destroy Ephraim;
> for I am God and not man,
>   the Holy One in your midst,
>   and I will not come to destroy.
>
>   (Hos. 11:1–2, 7–9)

Apparently God has his problems too. Should he follow a hard- or soft-line approach with his people? Should the church consist only of the hard-core, or is there a place for the soft-core as well?

In reality, the church has divided up along "hard" and "soft" denominational lines. Within Protestantism, the fundamentalist and evangelical denominations have demanded much of their members in allegiance, time, and money. The mainline denominations (Methodists, Episcopalians, Lutherans, United Church of Christ, Presbyterians, and so on) have demanded much less, and, it may be added parenthetically, they have received much less.

The Roman Catholic Church has traditionally been a hard-core denomination, but at the present time it is becoming softer and softer. I am amazed at some of the things that Roman Catholics say and do now as compared to twenty-five years ago. Even though I was never a Roman Catholic, I used to be ultrarespectful, if not semiterrified, of a priest. I think many Roman Catholics felt the same way. Now I have the feeling that priests are quite possibly normal mortals, who put their pants on one leg at a time like everyone else. Why, I even could say that some of my best priests are *friends.*

Although I have never known many Orthodox Christians personally, it is my impression that there is perhaps more fluidity in the Orthodox branch of the church than in either Roman Catholicism or Protestantism. That is, some national Orthodox churches are hard-core and some are soft-core. They have room for everyone, and if someone doesn't fit in one place, he or she can fit someplace else.

In any case, the most rigid denominations at times must be flexible, and the most flaccid denominations sometimes must become as hard as steel. In order to survive, the church must be both hard and soft.

Therefore we shall again pose the question with which this chapter began. Is the church of Jesus Christ like a peach, or is it like a banana? Is it supposed to be hard- or soft-core?

I am certain of this: the church cannot be like either an onion or a head of lettuce. You peel off the layers of an onion or a head of lettuce, and all you ever find is more layers, until at last there is nothing left.

The church isn't like that. The church has an essential *something,* and that something is both hard and soft, hard toward sin and soft toward sinners.

You know what is the best simile for the church? The church is like a pineapple. The soft part of the church is the nicer part, but there can be no sweet outer ring without a pulpy, hard inner core. You don't get one without the other. The hard part, which holds it all together, is one half of what it's all about. The soft part, which is what attracts most people, is the other half of what it's all about.

Hard *and* soft: that's what it's all about.

3:

The Fortress
vs.
The Front Line

In 1839, Bishop A. Cleveland Coxe of the American Episcopal Church wrote the text for a stirring hymn. It presents the church in the imagery of an impregnable fortress.

> O where are kings and empires now
>   Of old that went and came?
> But, Lord, Thy Church is praying yet,
>   A thousand years the same.
>
> We mark her goodly battlements,
>   And her foundations strong;
> We hear within the solemn voice
>   Of her unending song.
>
> For not like kingdoms of the world
>   Thy holy Church, O God;
> Though earthquake shocks are threatening her,
>   And tempests are abroad,
>
> Unshaken as eternal hills,
>   Immovable she stands,
> A mountain that shall fill the earth,
>   A house not made with hands.

Isn't that a rouser? What confidence, what assurance, what abiding faith is represented by that hymn!

But note: the underlying theme of the hymn is the image of the church as a fortress. A fortress is not an army that moves out against the enemy. It is a bastion which the enemy moves against. For Bishop Coxe, the church was the castle of God, bravely holding out against a hostile world which throughout the centuries had battered the church with the forces of secular paganism.

There is, however, another way of looking at the church. Instead of seeing it as God's fortress which the world is constantly trying to overthrow, one may envision the church as God's army, which is constantly trying to overthrow the world.

That's the way the Rev. Sabine Baring-Gould of the Church of England saw it. He also wrote the words for a stirring hymn, the tune for which, incidentally, was composed by Arthur Sullivan, one half of the team of Gilbert and Sullivan.

The year was 1865, just twenty-six years after "O Where Are Kings and Empires Now." But Father Baring-Gould perceived the church in an entirely different light. It was not a group of troops huddled behind the turrets; it was a company of commandos out there on the front lines.

> Onward, Christian soldiers,
>   Marching as to war,
> With the cross of Jesus
>   Going on before;
> Christ the Royal Master
>   Leads against the foe;
> Forward into battle,
>   See, His banners go.
>
> (Refrain)
> Onward, Christian soldiers,
>   Marching as to war,
> With the cross of Jesus
>   Going on before.

Like a mighty army
  Moves the Church of God;
Brothers, we are treading
  Where the saints have trod;
We are not divided,
  All one body we,
One in hope and doctrine,
  One in charity.
(Refrain)

Crowns and thrones may perish,
  Kingdoms rise and wane,
But the Church of Jesus
  Constant will remain;
Gates of hell can never
  'Gainst that Church prevail;
We have Christ's own promise,
  And that cannot fail.
(Refrain)

When I was growing up, there was no hymn I liked to sing more than "Onward, Christian Soldiers." For all I know, it may have been one of those powerful subconscious forces which made me want to be a minister when every other self-respecting young lad had decided to become a fireman or a railroad engineer. I didn't want to drive a fire truck or a steam locomotive; no, sir. I wanted to be an officer in an army, the army of God!

Well, I could say a few things that I've discovered about the shock troops of the Lord in the intervening years since my impressionable youth. But I won't. At least not now.

Instead I will make a historical observation: for more than half of its 1900-plus years of existence, the church of Jesus Christ has thought of itself primarily as God's Fortress, not his Front Line. In military terms, we were running a defensive war, not an offensive one.

This is not to say that there have been only two basic

phases of the war, one defensive, the other offensive. Actually, the nature of our warfare with the world has swung back and forth throughout history. In general, however, the church set out to conquer the world up until the fall of the Roman Empire and later the phenomenal growth of Islam. Then its primary objective was to keep from being conquered by the world.

The whole medieval period, from roughly A.D. 500 to 1500, was the period of the Fortress Church. The Front Line Church operated from A.D. 30 to 500, and again from 1500 to the present time.

As has been stated, though, it is really not so simple as that. For there were Fortress Christians in the early centuries, and Front Line Christians in the medieval centuries, and there have been many Fortress Christians since the Renaissance and the Reformation.

In the fifth century, for example, there lived a most unusual Christian whom the church has dubbed Simeon Stylites, or, as we might say, Simeon on a Stick. Old Simeon decided that the world was an evil place that could only corrupt him, so he went out into the Syrian desert and built himself a little house on top of a pillar. There he stayed the rest of his life. He became his own fortress against the contagion of life.

In the Middle Ages, the primary thrust of the church was toward monasticism, which represented the fortress type of thinking. Monastics such as St. Francis of Assisi and St. Thomas Aquinas were among the few bright lights shining in the medieval darkness. In the midst of this there was a vivid if somewhat sordid chapter in Front Line Christianity, called the Crusades. European armies set out on several occasions to retrieve the Holy Land from the Muslims, whom they derisively called "infidels." Not surprisingly, the Muslims returned the compliment, and in their vocabulary the Christians were the ones who were the infidels. If "infidel" means unfaithful, we would have to say that neither side was very faithful to God, and the amount of blood spilled in Palestine in those years made it anything but the Holy Land.

Since the Reformation and the Era of Front Line Christianity, there have been numerous Fortress Christians, among them Anabaptists, Shakers, Hutterites, Doukhobors, Mennonites, the Amish, and many of the Roman Catholic cloistered orders. They have stayed pretty much to themselves, and have deliberately tried to avoid contact with the outside world.

To be sure, out-and-out Fortress Christians are rare in these days. Yet the concept of the church as a fortress is by no means erased from our consciousness. We can see it in the very name of the large room in which most Christians worship on Sunday. What is it called? The sanctuary. And what is a sanctuary? It is a refuge, a place of safety, a fortress in which one is immune from the cares and pressures and concerns of the world.

We see the conflict in our approach to corporate worship. What is the function of worship? Is it simply to praise God? Is it to provide a spiritual refill for Christians who are on the busy road of life? Is it to equip people to be more effective soldiers for Christ in a world that opposes the Christian gospel? Should worship be that sweet-hour-of-prayer experience which grants men and women solace from a busy world when it appears they can find peace and comfort in no other way?

I find that people have some pretty definite ideas about what they want to hear in preaching. If I emphasize too much involvement in the world for too long a time, the devotees of personal religion let me know that they need to hear something about how God is present in their lives as Affirmer and Comforter and as Guardian of the Fortress. If I stress inner religion too much for too long, the Front Line Brigade and the Army of Evangelicals serve notice that they want instructions on how to leap into the thick of the worldly fray and overcome the forces of darkness and how to speak a good word for Jesus.

A preacher who took either of these comments too seriously would become totally discouraged or totally in- capacitated. As it is, we should take heart. At least such com- ments show that the troops are listening, and they know that they aren't getting what they want. So it behooves the minis- ter to serve a balanced diet of homiletical vitamins, given the limitations of the cooking school attended and the denomina- tion's spiritual nutrition tables.

But let us return more specifically to the nature of the church with respect to the world. Should the church be a place for spiritual R & R (rest and relaxation) for its soldiers, or should it be a training school for rangers and airborne candidates?

Though the past four and a half centuries have been char- acterized by the Front Line approach, among both Roman Catholics and Protestants, the present trend is back toward the church as a Fortress, at least in the American church. This is especially true among many suburban churches. The attitude is typified by the oft-used phrase, "It's a jungle out there!" Commuting to work by rail or automobile is a jungle, the world of work is a jungle, and many times life at home is a jungle.

If that is the way one feels, what is wanted from the church? Such a person wants peace, quiet, and reassurance. One would like to know that the world, which is perceived as a threatening reality, shall not swallow one up. In short, one longs to hear the words of Jesus: "Fear not, little flock, I have overcome the world."

When the world is understood as a jungle, and one fears sinister tribesmen stealthily sneaking around with their poi- soned darts and their perilous pink termination slips, one wants the church to be a chapel. And many suburban churches have become just that. Battered commuters and their station wagon spouses go to church in hopes of finding meaning for their frazzled lives. It is travel that breaks the spirit of suburbanites, travel to and from work, to and from the shopping center, to and from meetings, to and from an unlimited number of youth activities. The church is conceived to be the antidote, the defense, the fortress against all that.

In the late '50s and in the '60s, it was popular to disparage the suburban church-as-chapel. Probably it is still popular in some circles. But with a modicum of reflection it is easy to see how the church came to project that image. People's lives were being stretched too far by the very things that led people to the suburbs—green grass and space. They had to pass too much green grass and too much open space to get to where they had to be. The getting there was *getting* them. And they wanted Christianity to become a fortress.

City folks, on the other hand, generally don't take nearly as long to get where they are going. What they see on the way may be less pleasant (mounds of garbage, graffittied walls and subway cars, steaming ghettos), but at least it is a conscious reality with which one lives, while the suburbanite's travel time is usually a subconscious reality that he is not even aware of.

Because the urban dweller is continuously exposed to the seamier side of the environment by sight, sound, taste, touch, and smell, he or she wants the church to be involved in overcoming the world. A police barricade is the front line, the army of God is called into action at Fifth Avenue and 52d Street or at State and Madison or at Hollywood and Vine, and when the roll is called down yonder, they'll be there. You don't find many of the-church-is-the-church-and-the-world-is-the-world-and-never-the-twain-shall-meet type of fundamentalists in the city. For city folks there may be a pie in the sky by and by, but there's also a blockbusting realtor operating in the neighborhood and they want his by-glory backside kicked out of their turf immediately if not sooner and the church is as likely a prospect to do the kicking as anything else, so let's get with it, Christians.

What about *your* church? Is it a fortress, or is it at the front line? Look at your church's weekly calendar of events and you'll have a good part of the answer to the question. What kinds of meetings do you hold in your church building? Are the meetings only for your own members, or are they for the community as well? And what kinds of community groups do you allow to meet at your church? Are your programs designed to *fortify* your members (a key word), or do they train them for action?

Or look at your church budget. How do you spend your money? What percentage of the budget is internal, for the congregation only, and what percentage is used externally for the work of the church beyond the parish itself?

Look at your calendar and look at your budget, and you'll have a pretty good idea whether your church is an army unit that is holding down the fort or one that finds itself at the front line. Be clear about this: either way you can get killed. But there are two distinctly different types of battles that are being fought, depending upon whether your church is a castle with ramparts and turrets and thick walls and a moat or a collection of recruits out in the streets and in the bullet-scarred buildings and in the no-man's-land of the city park where the shots are coming from all sides and it's hard to tell who is enemy and who is friend.

You might assume you should favor one concept of the church over the other, that the church should be a Front Line unit rather than a Fortress unit, or vice versa. Not so. It depends on the circumstances. Before one can decide, one must investigate the situation in which the church finds itself.

Where is your church located? At what point in time is it located there? What are the conditions of the world around you? What is the condition of the Christians among you?

Let's look at some specific illustrations.

If Peter, Paul, Barnabas, and Company had decided that the church should be a fortress, they would have gone out of business in about three hours. At the time they lived, hardly anyone was a Christian. So how could they possibly have held out against the world? The world would have smashed their little sand castle in nothing flat. Aggressively, sometimes abrasively, they went from Jerusalem into every corner of the Roman Empire to recruit new troops. They couldn't wait around for soldiers to join their army; their army went out to join the soldiers. They had a slogan—"The Army Wants to Join You"; it was very clever. Twentieth-century Madison Avenue couldn't do any better.

By the year 500, however, the church had grown so large and had acquired so much political and spiritual power that it could afford to prepare for a thousand-year siege. Perhaps it had no other real choice, any more than the early church had had any choice other than the front line. Ignorance was going to bombard the church; Islam and paganism and internal stupidity were going to test the church severely. Maybe its only alternative was to stop and dig trenches and throw up fortifications and slog it out right there in western and central Europe for a millennium. It was nasty—but it may have been necessary.

What kind of church should the church be today? That depends on which church in which part of the world you're talking about. The church in South Korea can't be a fortress. It has to go to the front lines and carry the battle to the enemy, because it is a battle it can win, and the offensive method is probably the only one it can use to win it. The church in China or the Soviet Union can't be either a fortress or a front line; it has to be a tunnel. It has to go underground, and meet in secret. The church in Rhodesia or South Africa or Uganda or parts of South America will one day need to be a fortress, the next day a platoon of paratroopers who drop behind the enemy lines. The church in Europe lost out at the front lines long ago, and hasn't fared well as a fortress either. So maybe European Christians should start training some shock troops to go out into the highways and byways again. They did it successfully eighteen hundred years ago.

In North America, the pattern is a patchwork quilt. A dying church in a decaying city neighborhood doesn't have the option of trying to be a fortress. It has to move the battle to the streets and the tenements. A suburban church which has grown large and has become part of the establishment may have to become fortresslike for a time as the social upheavals of the '60s settle into the quiet personal probings of the '70s. In the towns and villages and open country of the heartland, congregations may have the luxury of being both a fortress and at the front line. Where the church is still widely accepted in a community yet is still free from being identified inseparably with the community, it can choose whichever method of warfare it wants and whenever it wants that kind of war.

●   ●   ●

It is certain that some of you will find the language of the military with reference to the church quite—you should pardon the expression—*offensive*. Why must we think of the church as an army at all? Haven't "O Where Are Kings and Empires Now" and "Onward, Christian Soldiers" both had their hymnodic as well as theological day?

For some that is undoubtedly true. It is repugnant to their concept of the church that Christians should ever be conceived as soldiers, and they feel embattled whenever the tendency appears to be recurring. This militaristic language especially galls them when they recall that in this century soldiers have killed scores of millions of human beings in a series of increasingly bloody wars.

Besides, it could be pointed out, the Salvation Army and the Society of Jesus are the only genuine vestiges of the military-religious left within Christianity. And the iron discipline of the old days is even beginning to crumble in them. The rest of us are like a squad of Girl Scouts.

That may be. But it only raises another means of seeing the polarity which exists in the church, and which has always existed. It is the issue of the Marshmallow Church *vs.* the Militant Church.

Must the church be tender, or must it be tough? Can it be both? Can it be both at the same time?

Discipline has been slipping in most nonfundamentalist denominations for the past several years, just as it has also ebbed in many families in many Western nations in the past generation. Does it really surprise anyone that it is those denominations which are organized along military lines which are making some of the most publicized progress just now—Mormons, Jehovah's Witnesses, Seventh-day Adventists, the Unification Church, and the like? In those churches, if someone in authority tells you to do or believe something, you do or believe it, because you follow orders.

Leo Durocher, who by his own admission was never one of the nicest guys ever to manage a baseball team, issued the famous dictum, "Nice guys finish last." The church needs to think about whether it wants to win or be nice, be militant or be a marshmallow, be an army or not, and if it does, whether it wants to fight a defensive or an offensive battle.

Such a decision can never be unanimous. We should expect that the decision will be divisive. But a decision should be made. To choose will cause warfare in the church. Not to choose will cause warfare in the church.

All signs point to war.

What is your choice?

4:

The Arrived

vs.

The Arriving

A town of 20,000 in northern Illinois. Not the Bible Belt; too far north. But not too far up yonder to be beyond the reach of Old-Time Religion.

An itinerant evangelist has come to town. This is no slicker-than-goose-grease, well-oiled operation; this is straight stuff, no smoothness, electronic organ, three hundred battle-scarred folding chairs type of tent Christianity.

A slice of Americana is to be seen here. Although it is farming country, these farmers are no rustic rubes. At a thousand dollars an acre (it is 1961), you must be shrewd and astute to succeed in these early days of agribusiness.

Nevertheless, there are no airs about the people in this Bible-believing itinerant's ersatz congregation. They drift in by twos and threes, clean, but not elegant. Those few men who have worn coats on this hot July evening have not bothered to complete the effect with a well-coordinated necktie; a bolo tie will suffice, if any neckwear is to be worn at all. The women are in dresses (no slacks), and the children, what few of them there are, are freshly scrubbed, laundered, pressed, and squirming.

The time for beginning the service, like the manner of the evangelist, is fluid. It is supposed to start at eight o'clock, but at eight o'clock there are precious few souls to be saved. The preacher is hoping, not for a bigger crowd, but for anything that resembles a crowd. By eight twenty-five, a scant hundred have assembled, and he begins.

There is singing. These people know the hymns by heart. Millions of Christians have never laid ears on these tunes before, but other millions have. The hot July Illinois evening congregation are part of the others. Though few in number, they belt them out. They practically drown out the electronic organ, which in normal circumstances is not a consummate sin, and in this instance seems a moral and musical act of righteousness.

There are prayers, and Scripture readings, and announcements. And also Amens. When you aren't used to them, Amens are at once fascinating and frightening.

Then the sermon. The evangelist begins by using a by now forgotten biblical text. He starts softly and builds slowly. What he is concerned about is sin. And repentance. Word by word, paragraph by paragraph, point by bludgeoned point, he builds up to the climax. He takes his time. One wonders if he has done all of this before, many, many times before.

Then it comes, the curiously still remembered homiletic punch line, "You may be sure . . . [pause], you may be absolutely sure . . . [pause], you may be absolutely sure beyond the shadow of a doubt that the Lord will find you out!"

It matters not that if you're sure, you don't need to be *absolutely* sure, and if you're absolutely sure, you *are* sure beyond the shadow of a doubt; he isn't the first preacher in the world to use verbal overkill, nor will he be the last. The point is this: the canvas evangelist was talking about a theological and especially an emotional reality of which his congregation was aware, and they hung on every Old-Time Religion word.

There were ninety-nine who were of the preacher's fold that night, and one lost sheep who never saw the likes of it before or since. He was a young Presbyterian who in two months' time would be a student in a Presbyterian seminary, and in three years would be a Presbyterian minister. He thought as part of his education between the university and the seminary he should see what an old-fashioned tent meeting was all about. Well, he saw, and the tent preacher saw him. No doubt that soon-to-be seminarian had a bewildered, what-in-heaven's-name-is-going-on-here look in his eyes, and he must have stuck out like a Peruvian peasant watching his first game of ice hockey.

This evangelist and everyone else except the Presbyterian, who recognized no other Presbyterians, or anyone else for that matter, all shared something in common. They had an apparent certainty about them, in their faces and in their manner. They knew they were saved. When asked to come forward to dedicate themselves to Jesus Christ, a few did, but it seemed evident that they were used to going forward. Besides, they believed, correctly I presume, that it made the evangelist feel good. They had *arrived,* these Christians. And they knew it.

But there was one of whom the evangelist could not be certain, whose timidity kept him glued to his chair, the young man who didn't know the hymns and was ill at ease, but who tried unsuccessfully to mask it. To him the preacher went first when he was finished with his sermon, as the fly to the overripe apple—or as the tiger to the bound and bleating sheep tied firmly to the hunter's stake.

Looking him straight in the eye, the evangelist queried the young man, "Are you saved?" And the young man, trying to look back just as uncrookedly, said, "Yes, sir; I am."

Was it "YES, SIR; I AM!" or "yessir i am"? The panic of the moment and the mists of the intervening years have obfuscated the nuance of the answer.

In any case, the answer was false. It was an attempted deception. That is, it may be true that the young man was and is saved, but he didn't know it for sure. He only wanted to avoid what he assumed would be an embarrassing, indeterminate, and ultimately fruitless argument. He knew that he had not arrived in God's kingdom in the same way that the evangelist and his constituents had arrived, and he suspected he would never have that feeling. So he said, "Yes, sir; I am saved" with as much conviction as he could muster. He left both the evangelist and himself disappointed with his answer.

•   •   •

A couple of years later that same seminary student, about whose identity the reader may have some strong suspicions, was in a seminar discussion with a group of his classmates and an able and articulate professor. The seminar was entitled "Justification and Sanctification." It was a course offered by the Church History Department of the seminary.

Somehow the question of the knowledge of one's own salvation arose. Here it was all heady and academic. But it was the same basic question that had been asked at the tent meeting, "Are you saved?"

Perhaps it might be shocking to some, but the participants in the discussion were about evenly divided on their answers. As I recall, no one was confident that he would be eternally unsaved, but some were certain of their salvation, while others were not. I was in the latter group.

The professor, a great admirer of Martin Luther, reminded us that Luther said we should know we are saved, and if Luther said it, it must be so.

His pedagogical protégés, those of us in the Non-Knowers camp, suggested that Calvin had hypothesized that no one except God knew who was saved, to which the professor, originally an English Methodist, responded with a definitely mirthful "Humph!" The debate continued for some time, but with that humph it essentially was terminated.

Never underestimate the power of the humph. It is a wondrous weapon in the ecclesiastical arsenal.

•   •   •

In the church of Jesus Christ, there are two kinds of people: the Arrived and the Arriving. That is, there are those who are certain they belong, that God loves them, and that they have fulfilled the basic requirements of what it is to be a Christian. And then there are those who think and hope that they belong and that God loves them, but they have doubts about their having fulfilled the basic requirements for becoming subjects in the kingdom of God. Is their faith strong enough? Is their understanding deep enough? They lack certainty. Probably we should mention a third category: those who belong to the church in name, but who in fact for reasons of conscience feel that they should not belong at all. They are, however, a separate consideration, and do not fit into the polarity suggested by this chapter. Please humor the author, especially if you are in the third category.

In general, fundamentalists and theological conservatives, at least the outspoken ones, tend toward the Arrived category. You don't need to ask Pentecostals, Seventh-day Adventists, Mormons, or Southern Baptists if they have been saved; you know they will tell you that they have. Ask an Episcopalian, a Methodist, a Presbyterian, or even many American Baptists the same question, and you may hear some hedging. *Maybe* they are saved, they certainly hope they are saved, but they are not certain. Ask the most liberal of Episcopalians, Presbyterians, *et al.* that question, and along with the Unitarians and the Reformed Jews, they will ask, "What do you mean by this strange word 'saved'?"

The issue of Arrived *vs.* Arriving arises when people join a church. There is much more movement from one denomination to another than there used to be, and frequently new members will ask, "What must I believe to be a member of this church?"

That query may imply many things, such as:

> *Intellectual curiosity.* "Just what is it that Presbyterians (or whatever) believe, anyway?"

> *Theological propriety.* "If I'm going to be a member of this church, I want to affirm what it affirms."

Personal integrity. "Can I be honest in joining this church, believing the things I do, questioning the things I question, doing the things I do?"

Existential uncertainty. "If I feel that my life up to this point is more of a pilgrimage or a quest than it is a matter of having made some startling discoveries, do I have any business joining a church in the first place?"

For many persons, certainty of salvation and the feeling that one has arrived result from what has been called "a conversion experience." Some denominations encourage conversion experiences by means of altar calls, emotional appeals, and unabashed religious promotion and salesmanship. Some denominations almost insist on a conversion experience as a means of validating the genuineness of a person's faith.

Mainline Protestants in the late twentieth century have become less and less comfortable with conversion experiences. These spiritual highs are not denied, but they are not promoted either. We have concluded that the sawdust trail is a thing of the past. For us, the road to heaven is paved with a more cohesive surfacing material, keeping our shoes free from the telltale film of dusty emotionalism.

We have paid a price for that. Fewer of our people are convinced of their salvation. They doubt that they have arrived; they even wonder if they are arriving.

In his reference to the sheep and the goats (Matt. 25: 31–46), Jesus indicated that those who follow him (the sheep) would be with him in his kingdom, while those who didn't follow him (the goats) would be cast out into eternal punishment. Those who are convinced that they are sheep clearly feel they have arrived. Those who are not so convinced might assume they are goats.

Sheep have more fun. They graze in green pastures beside still waters. Goats are to be found in scruffy landfills beside city dumps chomping on tin cans and old shoes, suffering the pains of heartburn and gas. They are also the victims of the unpredictable belch. Goats never feel that they have arrived, and question whether they are arriving. Somehow the city dump does not seem to be where it's all at to the goats of this world.

How do you separate the sheep from the goats? You don't have to. They separate themselves. The sheep stand on one side, firmly believing that they are belly deep in divinely provided chlorophyll, and they remind the other half that they are not standing in grass but in the wretched refuse of the world's polluting populace. The goats don't see it quite that way, but they do see themselves more as sows' ears than as silk purses.

Needless to say, the voluntary separation into two groups, the Arrived and the Arriving, or the Sheep and the Goats, can create attitudes of superiority and inferiority in the church. It is another example of the war within. Those who believe that they now are as God meant them to be can feel soiled by the presence of those who have not attained such high standards. And those who do not claim to be the Christians they know they should be may feel ignored, shunned, or frozen out by the more virtuous church members who possess the proper spiritual pedigree.

Sometimes the question is focused by poignantly personal circumstances. In considering nominations for church officers, should nominating committees consider people who are divorced, who have been convicted of crimes or misdemeanors, or who have any degree of notoriety clinging to their past? Should alcoholics, compulsive gamblers, or homosexuals be rejected, even though they may exhibit extraordinary skills and faithfulness otherwise?

Or what is a church governing board or pastor to do if someone expresses an interest in joining the church who is a known philanderer, or adulterer? Or who engages in business dealings that are known to be as shady as the Amazon jungle on a moonless night? What then?

Is the church for the Arrived or the Arriving—or both? Is there a minimum standard of conduct that must be decreed, or simply a minimum statement of faith? And who should make the determination?

Whoever it is who decides, a decision must be made. Officials within the church decide. Church members decide. People wanting to be church members decide. People who are as interested in joining the church as they would be in volunteering to be guinea pigs for a new drug designed to cure hives but with potential side effects of hangnails or heart attacks also decide. Furthermore, as has been stated by somebody or other, not to decide is to decide.

Whether inside or outside the church, people have definite opinions on what Christians are supposed to be, and whether or not anyone has yet measured up to those criteria. Obviously millions feel they have, else they could not in good conscience continue as church members. Other millions believe that though they have not attained what they have set up for themselves as the authentic marks of the Christian life, they are nevertheless attempting to incorporate those marks into their being. "Forgetting what lies behind and straining forward to what lies ahead, I press on toward the goal for the prize of the upward call of God in Christ Jesus" was the way the apostle Paul described it (Phil. 3:13–14).

Part of the animosity which may develop between the Arrived and the Arriving comes in a basic disagreement over the meaning of arrival. I distinctly remember a discussion a number of years ago in an adult Christian education class. There was a man there who had some decidedly fundamentalist tendencies, and who later took the plunge into the most rigid of fundamentalism. The discussion centered on the question of arriving as a Christian, though it was couched in different terms.

The man proposed that perfection was the goal for every Christian, and that when we attain perfection, then we can claim to be true followers of Jesus Christ. The class, respectful of the gentleman but hardly partisans of his, objected that perfection was beyond man's capability. Coming to the same conclusion as Browning, but from a different angle, "or what's a heaven for?" seemed to be the thrust of their argument. If we are perfectible, then let's skip heaven entirely; earth itself will be quite sufficient, thank you.

"Yes, but," retorted the man (the war within the church is punctuated by countless Yes Buts), "it is possible to become 97 or 98 or 99 percent perfect, isn't it?" Not wanting to press him further, the class relented, for though they did not agree with the man, they liked him.

There is still a major flaw in his argument. To be 97 or 98 or 99 percent perfect is a contradiction in terms. Perfection comes in only one percentage number, and that is 100 percent. Anything less than that is less than perfect, and thus by definition is not perfect. It is like saying that a guided missile fired at a target a hundred miles down range which misses by only two miles is 98 percent perfect. Translate that into a volley against Moscow in case of war, and the missile may come down anywhere between Warsaw and Novosibirsk.

When all is said and done, "Arrived" and "Arriving" are subjective concepts. One man's arriving is another man's arrived. This man's Expert is that man's Beginner. The apostle Paul, who wrote to the Philippians about pressing on toward the goal of the call of Christ, was a good bit more advanced than the coat-toting coward who cheered as Stephen was stoned to death or even than the man knocked from his horse on the Damascus road, however real his conversion was.

If ever we are to overcome the friction that can arise because of trying to decide who is or is not already a part of God's kingdom, we must learn to be more tolerant, allowing for a flexible set of ground rules. This means that the Arriveds must concede that those whom they feel have not yet gotten there are nevertheless on the way. And the Arrivings must concede the Arriveds the right to their opinion that they have arrived, even though they may question the veracity of that opinion themselves. Keeping the lines of communication open, in the church as in marriage, can work wonders toward deeper and more mature relationships.

5:

God's Democracy

vs.

God's Bureaucracy

The church is a truly remarkable institution. In one sense it is and has been the only genuinely democratic institution that ever existed. Sitting side by side in the same pew on a Sunday morning might be an immigrant day laborer and a Pulitzer Prize-winning journalist. Serving as ushers there might be a so-called captain of industry (Why is it that industry has only captains? They seem more like generals or field marshals) and a man who never rose above the lower middle ranks as a dedicated civil service employee. On the same church board one might find a famous socialite known for the who'swhoedness of her friends and acquaintances and a shy spinster secretary who has a commitment to the cause of Christ which is as radiant as the sun on a crystal day in autumn.

Of course there is stratification in the church. There are different strata of churches, and different strata of people within churches. Still, the church generally cuts across and encompasses each stratum much better than any other centuries-old institution.

No other organization is able to help so many people so quickly with such low overhead. Years ago a statistic was quoted by church officials to the effect that one dollar contributed to a well-known and well-publicized national agency would buy twenty pounds of food for starving people.

That same dollar given to that denomination's disaster relief fund would buy *three hundred* pounds of food. Those amounts could not be purchased now for the same cost because of inflation, but the same incredible disparity of buying power exists now.

And why? Because the church uses less costly means of publicity, spends far less on administration, and pays lower salaries than most other helping agencies.

The church is what businessmen would call a "labor intensive" organization. This means that a high percentage of the money its constituents contribute ("revenue" to management moguls) goes to pay salaries. Even a goodly chunk of the "mission" budget of a congregation is used for paying somebody to do something for somebody "out there" or "over there." But it gets done with surprisingly little waste and almost no graft. Compare that to either government or business.

The church exists for people. It is a fellowship of people whose efforts, concerns, and prayers are for men, women, and children everywhere. If the church ever loses sight of the fact that it is centered primarily on people, even more than programs, it will cease to exist.

Late one evening a famous theological professor received a telephone call from one of his students, who asked to see him immediately. The theologian was in the midst of deep thought, and he wanted to carry his thought through to its conclusion. He wondered if the student might wait until morning. Politely and calmly the student said that he would. The professor went back to his thoughts. The student went and put a bullet through his head. It was a tragic reminder of a truth the sensitive theologian had long known, but which momentarily he forgot: people must come first.

The church, which is God's democracy, has remembered pretty well. That doesn't mean that most of us can't recall instances where the church failed us as individuals. A pastor was inattentive at a time of crisis or need, an officer in a church organization said or did something improper at some point along the line, a church member was catty or cutting or unkind. But if we are objective, most of us would admit that in general we have been treated with greater courtesy, respect, and consideration by church members than by non-church people.

There is an essential dignity and integrity in most church people. When they understand what the church is, and why the Lord has called it into being, they *care.* They care about others, about their relationship to others, about giving others an opportunity to express themselves within the fellowship of believers.

Great Scott, isn't the church wonderful!

•   •   •

And *then* there's the other side of the coin. On the one hand the church is God's blessed democracy. Then again it is God's blasted bureaucracy. The voice of the people is lost in the cacophony of officials, official pronouncements, bureaucracy, and bureaucrats.

Sometimes we live with an illusion. It is the fond hope that always and in every instance the church can and will be sensitive to human dilemmas and to cries for help and comfort.

The Roman Catholic Church presents itself as the best illustration of the church of and for people *vs.* the institutional juggernaut, since it is the largest and rightfully the most publicized communion within the Christian family. Take the issue of birth control. Here is something of vital concern, not only to Roman Catholics but to the whole world. The population explosion, changing patterns in marriage and family life, and a worldwide sexual revolution all create tremendous pressures for some renewed thinking on the traditional teachings of Mother Church with respect to birth control.

So what happens? Over in Rome there is an octogenarian

Italian surrounded by a whole crowd of other octo- and sep-
tuagenarian Italians. (Did it ever seem odd to you to realize
how many Italian cardinals there are? The Roman Curia
reads like a page from the Rome telephone book. Half a
billion Roman Catholics worldwide, maybe one twentieth of
them Italians, and half the Curia comes from Italy. Very
interesting.)

Anyway, this octogenarian gentleman confers with other
elder statesmen of the church on the matter of birth control.
He knows some people think he's a reactionary, while others
think he's a radical—not many, but some. But it is a trifle
ludicrous for a group of aged celibates, albeit learned and
able, to come up with a satisfactory statement on birth control. It is like a conference of Orthodox rabbis trying to decide what is the best way to cook a Virginia ham.

Yet the pope and his colleagues *must* take a stand. And
whatever position they take is going to alienate millions of
Roman Catholics. If they decide on a more liberal approach,
the conservatives will be scandalized. If they are too conservative, the liberals will be put off. Either way, the cry will go
up that the church (which means the bishop of all the bishops
of the church) is not sensitive to either the leading of the
Spirit or the will of the people. And the pope, poor, belea-
guered, lonely soul that his office forces him to be, says to
himself: "Well, I'm *dannato* if I do and *dannato* if I don't.
Why did I ever take this job in the first place? *Mamma mia!*"

How do *people* get lost in the bureaucratic shuffle that
leads to such agonizing decisions? Don't any of those men in
the red hats ever have their ears to the ground? Or is it that
the red hats cover their ears—or their minds?

Nevertheless, it is easy for us to criticize the pope or the
Curia or the Vatican or the hierarchy for their seeming indif-
ference to the great masses of the faithful. But it is something
else to be in a position of authority where decisions need to
be made, often without a proper amount of time to hear all
sides of a question.

The most striking example of this phenomenon from my own experience occurred on July 1, 1971. I will always remember the date, because our son Andrew was born the day before.

At that time I was one of three assistant ministers on the staff of the Fourth Presbyterian Church on North Michigan Avenue in Chicago. A group of American Indians from several tribes had occupied a Nike missile base a few miles north of the church on Chicago's lakefront. They wanted to draw attention to the plight of the Indian, especially the urban Indian.

For a few weeks the local and military authorities allowed the occupation of the missile base. Then suddenly, at dawn on July 1, they stormed through the chain link fences and drove the demonstrators out.

It happened that I had known the leader of the group when I had worked as a student assistant one summer in a church on a Chippewa reservation in northern Wisconsin. Whether that acquaintanceship was the factor which precipitated his next move I have never been sure. But the next thing we knew was that the whole group trooped into the church and announced that it was now Indian territory.

Try to picture this scene, if you will. None of the other ministers is in town, not one. The church executive and I are the only two people there who remotely resemble Persons in Authority. One minute everything is church business as usual, and the next minute thirty Indians—men, women, and children—are sitting on the floor around the reception desk, declaring that they have taken over the place. This is a city of three and a half million people. Across the street is a hundred-story building. There is no unit of the U.S. Cavalry nearby. Yet here are some gentlemen with headbands and feathers. We also have here a flabbergasted receptionist, four or five secretaries who don't know whether to be amused or worried, a couple of janitors for whom any unscheduled group is an unconscionable pain in the neck, and a church executive and an assistant minister who soon will be rolling around in their heads the notion that late June and early July would have been a splendid time to have gone on vacation. Tending toward the unusual, this. Even unique.

In retrospect there were elements of high comedy about that whole episode. Funny, but we didn't hear many laughs then.

The leader of the group said that they would occupy the church premises until four demands were met. They were that they receive: (1) food, which they badly needed; (2) medical care, which some needed; (3) housing, which only a few of this particular group needed as it turned out, but which many Indians in Chicago did need; and (4) legal representation, which, in the aftermath, none of them needed.

With a congregation of three thousand, we were able to call on some members who could supply them with all of their requests. (We chose to drop the emotional overtones of the word "demands" to the more prosaic and Presbyterian-sounding word "requests.") Within an hour or so some of our deacons brought in food. Two doctors were on the scene shortly thereafter, and administered any necessary medical assistance. Lawyers volunteered to represent the Indians if need be. By the next morning a member who worked for the Chicago Housing Authority had arranged for all thirty people to be housed. And when they made a fifth request (demand) of us, that we provide them transportation from the church as a group when they left, an executive with a bus firm ordered two buses to be placed at our disposal.

During the time the Indians were in the church building, which was about thirty hours, it was locked. Only those authorized to come in were allowed to enter. If any of the Indians left, they were told they would not be readmitted.

In the meantime, newspaper reporters and television crews were outside on the street, clamoring to know what was going on. They weren't the only ones; we were more than mildly interested in finding that out ourselves. Finally, a group of our elders and trustees agreed on a press release. They also agreed that I should read it.

That was the first time I had ever done such a thing. I also hope it is the last time I ever have to do such a thing. Article I of the Bill of Rights on the freedom of the press seems a dandy idea until you've gone through the birth of a son, experienced an Indian invasion, stayed up most of the night at church to attempt to keep things calm, pondered as deeply as you could in the face of rather trying circumstances what was a proper Christian approach given the situation, and then faced a battery of microphones, cameras, and legions of questions when you were so nervous you figured being struck by lightning might be a kind stroke of providence.

The gist of our press release was this: we had met every request that the demonstrators had made of us. We felt we had dealt fairly with them. In view of our positive response to them, we insisted that they leave the church building by that afternoon, or else we would have them evicted by police action. Thank heaven, they left peaceably on the buses provided for them.

Where was God's democracy in that? What we decided to do was a decision made by just a few people, by representatives of the representatives who had been elected by the congregation. Under those conditions a congregational meeting or even a special meeting of the session was impossible. We knew we would be in trouble with some people no matter what we did. Some of the fan mail we received later suggested we should have had the whole semi-ruly mob arrested immediately, though the language was considerably spicier than that. Other letters declared that it was unchristian of a church to deal so summarily and heartlessly with a needy segment of American society.

In the heat of that drama, which is but a miniscule drop in the ecclesiastical bucket compared to some of the enormous decisions facing Christ's church today, we tried to bring the light of the gospel as we saw it into a trying situation which no one, including, I believe, the Indians, really wanted. And although theological and spiritual considerations were present in our decision, *politics* was the primary concern.

Politics is the battleground upon which the church determines whether it is to be God's democracy or God's bureaucracy. I don't mean secular politics as practiced by governments and political parties; I mean church politics, ecclesiastical politics. "Man is by nature a political animal," said Aristotle. Ecclesiastical man is also a political animal. Never say that the church must be above politics. The church, as every other organization which wishes to perpetuate itself, is compelled to develop a politics of its own. Politics is the means by which institutions make decisions and then carry them out. Therefore the question for the church is not whether it should or should not have ecclesiastical politics; it *must* have a political system of some sort. The question is this: Is the necessary practice of church politics conducted well or poorly, fairly or unfairly, with intelligence or with stumbling, fumbling, bumbling ineptitude?

There are three basic forms of church government. Although there are variations from one congregation to another and from one denomination to another, all churches operate by using one of these three basic methods to govern themselves.

One system is the *episcopal* system (with a small "e"). This term comes from the Greek word *episkopos,* which means "bishop." In this form of church government, the primary center of ecclesiastical power resides in the office of the bishop. Though the bishop does not have unlimited authority, he is certainly the most powerful and influential person in his diocese, district, or conference. This system of government, incidentally, is the one followed by a strong majority of the world's Christians, including Roman Catholics, the various Eastern Orthodox churches, Methodists, Lutherans, and Anglicans or Episcopalians.

A second mode of church government is the *congrega-*

tional system (with a small "c"). Here, there is no hierarchy at all, or we might say that the local congregation itself is its own hierarchy. In other words, no individual or group outside the local church can order that congregation to do anything it does not want to do. The congregation elects officers, and those officers have certain responsibilities. But still it is the congregation as a whole who determine policy for the local church. The power is literally in the hands of the people, all the people.

In the fairly recently celebrated case of the First Baptist Church of Plains, Georgia, for example, a church now famous because it once had a famous member, the congregation took a vote on whether or not it would accept a black man into membership. The Southern Baptist Convention could not force that church to take any action one way or the other. If the convention were unhappy with the decision, it could remove the church from membership in the convention, but it could not rescind any action the congregation might have taken. Congregational government is the next most popular form of government in the worldwide Christian church. It is practiced by the various Baptist denominations, many of the fundamentalist and "evangelical" churches, and in the United States by the United Church of Christ, and elsewhere by those who call themselves Congregationalists.

A third mode of government is the *presbyterian* system (with a small "p"). This word comes from the Greek *presbuteros,* which means "elder." Here, every church so governed has a direct link with every other church in a given area, as in the episcopal system, but the geographical area is not called a diocese; it is called a presbytery, or classis. The presbytery and classis function as a collective bishop. That is, each church is represented at the presbytery or classis meetings by their minister or ministers and by an equal number of lay elders. The presbytery and classis make the same kinds of decisions and have the same powers as bishops, but it is collective power. Presbyterian government is used by the several Presbyterian denominations and by most of the churches of the Reformed tradition.

If you compare church government to civil government, it works out like this:

episcopacy = monarchy

congregationalism = pure democracy

presbyterianism = republican or representative
                 democracy

Now, let us return to the question of how the church exercises its necessary political process. Does it do it with success or with failure?

Politics exists in all three forms of church government. All three forms have advantages and disadvantages. They all are subject to human error and fallibility; "sin" is a word the church often uses to describe those failings.

None of the three basic forms of ecclesiastical government is *the* one intended for his church by God. If I am wrong on this, may God strike me dead. If this book ends right here, you know I was wrong. If not, you know (1) I was not wrong, or (2) God decided to nail me later on.

The New Testament is most inexplicit about how the church is to be governed. A case can be made for any of the three types, or for any combination of the three. Hard as it is to believe, it seems to come down to that sage folk dictum, "You pays your money and you takes your choice."

However, it behooves all of us to try to create the best and the most productive political climate possible in the governmental form into which we have paid our money. The church doesn't need *less* politics; it needs *better* politics. It needs people who really care, people who are lay persons, elected church officers, pastors, administrators, bishops, cardinals, popes, whatever.

One of our problems is that we may become the most intensely political about that which is the most inconsequential and when the stakes are the most insignificant, especially at the local level. A congregation or church board can become absolutely paralyzed by a decision over whether to contribute $50 to a full-page Council of Churches ad in the newspaper opposing the installation of a nuclear power station in Upper Volta, but they will spend $50,000 for a youth lounge with scarcely the blink of an ecclesiastical eye. (Discount that latter figure by 90 percent if it's a small church, double it if the congregation is a giant.)

Among the church membership at large, and even among many of the clergy, there can develop an "us" *vs.* "them" political syndrome. *We* are the ordinary people, and *they* are the churchly bureaucracy, the people "up there" or "over there," the people on church boards and agencies, or in diocesan or district offices, or in denominational headquarters.

Well, "they" are just "we" who went from "here" to "there." If we are unhappy with them, let's tell them why. Even bureaucrats can reform. No Christians are beyond the hope of redemption. In fact, you might even say that Christians believe in redemption, and that it has already happened.

Heaven knows it gets discouraging sometimes. Every pastor of a local church can testify to that. There is a constant battle of paper *vs.* people. The church exists for people, but many Christians seem to believe that it is fueled by paper, because every parson in any American church is sent enough mail in a week to choke the biblical leviathan, and you can also throw in the nonbiblical Trojan horse for good measure. If we read everything sent to us, we'd never see the earth in natural daylight or observe personally a single example of the species Homo sapiens for whom Christ died. Sometimes it appears that the church should quit the people business and go into the paper business. By controlling both the supply and the demand, we could get a good corner on the world market.

God's democracy *vs.* God's bureaucracy. People and politics. People *are* politics. Government requires bureaucracy, but it need not *be* bureaucracy.

May those of power in the church use their power wisely and well for the advancement of Christ's kingdom and the good of his servants. And if they don't, may those servants give them holy what-for until they do.

And in the meantime, may all of us survive this continuous battle between us and among us.

6:

The Spotless Bride

vs.

The Arbiter of Society

In the letter of James, a letter that Martin Luther said should be chucked forthwith out of the New Testament, the writer gives a description of what he believed to be true religion. "Religion that is pure and undefiled before God and the Father is this," said James, the brother of Jesus (purportedly), "to visit orphans and widows in their affliction, and to keep oneself unstained from the world." (James 1:27.)

It was the alleged "works righteousness" thesis that drove Dr. Luther up the wall. Luther's battle cry of the Reformation was, "Justification by Faith—Alone!"

In the verse quoted from this short New Testament epistle, there are tinges of the notion of salvation by works. But that isn't the main thing which concerns us in this verse. It is rather the advice "to keep oneself unstained from the world" that is the object of our perusal.

How do you suppose James might suggest we should accomplish that? Should we wear hip boots and rubber suits and hose ourselves down every night when we come home? Should we carry a giant economy-sized can of spot remover with us at all times? Should we stay in the house all the time so as to avoid earthly and earthy stains altogether?

Clearly no one could literally take James at his word. It is even difficult to follow his advice figuratively. If you live in the world at all, you're going to be stained by it. Sometimes you are going to get—how could we say it delicately?—guano on your Gucci boots and dung on your dungarees. It can't be helped.

Nevertheless, there are many Christians who feel that Christians in particular and the church in general should keep as pure and spotless and as untainted by the world as possible. This goal is implicit in one of the most beloved hymns of the past century.

> The Church's one Foundation
>   Is Jesus Christ her Lord;
> She is His new creation
>   By water and the word:
> From heaven He came and sought her
>   To be His holy Bride;
> With His own blood He bought her,
>   And for her life He died.

Here we have an image that goes back to New Testament times, that of the church as the spotless bride of Christ. Probably the idea originated in Jesus' parable of the wise and foolish virgins (Matt. 25:1–13). Christ is the bridegroom who at the least expected moment comes to claim his bride, which is to say, all those who are faithful to him, which is further to say, the church. Revelation expands on this notion when it says, "And I saw the holy city, new Jerusalem, coming down out of heaven from God, prepared as a bride adorned for her husband" (Rev. 21:2).

According to this view of the church, the people of God are those people who are in the world but not of it, who devote themselves wholly to the things of the Spirit, and refrain insofar as they are able from things of the flesh and of the world. And one thing in particular that they avoid is politics. Politics to them is a very dirty business.

Now there are a fair number of people the world over who are no more Christians than your average Arctic musk ox who also think that politics is a very dirty business. With the possible exception of Greece in the Golden Age, politicians have not enjoyed an unceasingly rosy reputation anywhere. Many people take an extremely dim view of politics. Far too many, in my opinion.

In the last chapter we referred to the necessity of church politics. If we could agree that politics is the system by which institutions make decisions and then carry out those decisions, we might even agree that church politics is necessary. But that is different, we might quickly interject. It's bad enough for Christians to have to become involved in Christian politics; it is unthinkable that they should enter into worldly politics too.

The history of the church with respect to attempts to affect the secular political process can be divided into three periods. For the first three hundred years everybody followed Paul's advice in Romans 13. "Let every person be subject to the governing authorities. For there is no authority except from God, and those that exist have been instituted by God," said Paul. (Rom. 13:1.) Whoever is in power is there by the direction of the Almighty. So keep your nose clean and stay out of trouble, Paul announces to us, and all will go well.

Then early in the fourth century one of our boys became the Roman emperor. When Constantine became a Christian, he ordered that Christianity was to be the religion of the whole Empire. A goodly number of Jews, along with some Zoroastrians, comfortable pagans, assorted animists, and agreeably apathetic folks, probably took issue with him. But one thing old Constantine had going for him was the Roman army, and that made a remarkable difference.

Anyway, that initiated the second period of the church vis-à-vis politics, which lasted for the next thousand years. It culminated in what the church came to call the Holy Roman Empire. No longer did the church try to remain aloof from secular politics. Now it *absorbed* secular politics. Whatever the church did was what the state did, and whatever the state did was what the church did. They worked hand in glove with each other. The church became the arbiter of society, and it determined the direction of men and of nations. Sometimes when you saw a public official, you couldn't tell by his manner of dress or speech whether he was a bishop or a burgomaster. Sometimes he was both in one.

Then along came the Protestant Reformation, which greatly confused the issue, though it did usher in the third period of the church in regard to politics. The best way to describe the third period is to say that it is a mixed bag. Some churches in some nations are intensely political; and other churches assiduously avoid politics altogether.

Roman Catholics in Italy and Spain for centuries worked very closely with the government. Then they withdrew somewhat, and at times in this century they have been quite cool if not overtly hostile to the governing authorities. Elsewhere where Roman Catholicism is strong, especially in Latin America and especially in the past ten years or so, there has been a growing antipathy between the church and the state. Many Roman Catholic laymen, priests, and bishops have spoken out loudly, even to the point of persecution and death, against the repressive military governments that have seized power with appalling frequency in some of the South and Central American countries.

During the Reformation, Luther took a pretty conservative stance. He stayed out of the affairs of state, though he gladly accepted the encouragement and protection of some of the pro-German, anti-Italian Germanic princes. Calvin thought the concept of the separation of church and state a most odious one, and was as imperious in his sixteenth-century Geneva as ever any pope was in medieval Rome. Much as I admire the Scots and the Church of Scotland, I would have to say that John Knox was more than slightly high-handed in the way he ruled both the ecclesiastical and temporal roosts once he became the chief laird of Caledonia. When you recall that Henry VIII declared the English monarch to be the earthly head of the church, you've remembered all you need to in order to understand how Hank viewed the theory of the separation of church and state.

Later on in the seventeenth century, the Congregationalists (or Puritans) were all for church involvement in affairs of state, so long as it was their church involved rather than someone else's, but the Methodists and Baptists were more standoffish. Politics was anathema to the Anabaptists and to many Quakers, and to this day the most orthodox of the Mennonites and Amish won't even send their children to public schools since they want to separate themselves completely from the public at large.

In short, the past five hundred years of church history have illustrated a wide variety of involvement or noninvolvement by churches in matters of the nation and politics. Historically, the issue is much less clear in our era than it has been in the other two periods of the church.

But *personally* for millions of individuals, and even for some denominations, the issue is crystal clear. Either the church is the Spotless Bride who is untainted by the world, or it is the Arbiter of Society. Either it should keep itself unstained, or it should be right in there pitching, trying to bring a strongly Christian perspective into the moral, ethical, social, and political concerns of the day.

If it is clear for individuals or denominations, it makes life much simpler. Then one does or does not get involved.

The problem is that for many of us, perhaps for most of us, it is not a clear issue. Instead it is confused and befuddling. Many Christians feel torn between staying out of politics because they are Christian or trying to effect policy for precisely the same reason. Were the so-called "German Christians" correct in going along with Hitler before and during World War II, or were the "Confessing Christians" following the proper course by not only opposing Hitler but seeking to kill him if they had an opportunity?

When religion or religious figures have been close to the center of political power, more often than not it seems to have had an unsavory influence. Attempts to create a theocracy generally deteriorate into an autocracy, and it is not God but some religious or irreligious megalomaniac who takes over the whole show.

History is generously sprinkled with instances of religion and politics combining to form a noxious chemical mixture. There was the brilliant Hildebrand, who became Pope Gregory VII, who forced Henry IV, the Holy Roman Emperor, to come to Canossa in the year 1077, there to march around the castle three days running barefoot in the snow. Not a very friendly fellow, Gregory, when he put the ecclesiastical screws to the powers that be who are ordained of God. The puritanical and ultrarighteous Oliver Cromwell destroyed half the great old churches in Britain when he came to power because they didn't happen to be the right kind of churches to suit his fancy. One of the most pungently mystifying of mystics in this or any other century was the wild-eyed Rasputin, the Russian monk who exercised an almost diabolical control over the last czar of all the Russias and his wife. Christianity can be a dangerous tool in the hands of those who possess political clout.

And yet examples also can be raised to support a union of Christian influence in politics. William Jennings Bryan was motivated in large measure by his Christian convictions. It is not without significance that the cross was the central image in his famous "Cross of Gold" speech. It did not, however, win him the presidency, even though he was three times a candidate for the office. Woodrow Wilson was a P.K. (preacher's kid), and his strong Calvinistic upbringing played a major part in shaping his political thought. The current President has not been bashful in declaring that Christian principles have influenced his political principles, and he testifies that they will continue to do so.

Countless individuals have entered the political arena specifically because of their Christian convictions. Daniel and Philip Berrigan, brothers who are Roman Catholic priests, have each taken bold action against the United States Government, particularly in the days of their opposition to the war in Vietnam. They both have served time in prison for their numerous endeavors.

In the 1960's, when public demonstrations were much more widely practiced and supported than they are now, lay persons and clergy could be seen carrying placards and trooping along in places all over the country. Many a congregation in many denominations was mightily proud or mightily upset—or both—that their pastor went down to Selma or city hall or somewhere else publicly to support or oppose something or other.

Nobody questions the right of *individuals* to take political or social stands on grounds of conscience. The wisdom of their stance might be questioned, but not their right to take it. And not many would deny the right of the church to try to inform and direct the conscience of individual Christians.

But what happens when the *church itself* takes a stand that has political overtones? One thing occurs for certain: it definitely does have a way of creating heat and static.

Many churches can come up with examples of dabblings in social and political stews, but nobody can cite a more controversial action than one taken several years ago by my own beloved and bewildering denomination, The United Presbyterian Church in the United States of America.

Angela Davis was on trial for an alleged crime. For those who don't know her, Angela Davis was one of the most publicized radicals of the '60s. She also was black. And an atheist. And a Communist.

In order to assist the legal defense of Miss Davis, a unit of an agency of the United Presbyterian Church contributed $10,000 to the Angela Davis Defense Fund, which it was later discovered needed money like the Sahara needs sand or like Carter needed little liver pills (an illustration for the more seasoned readers among you). Mind you, it was not the United Presbyterian Church itself that gave the money, but a unit of an agency of the United Presbyterian Church. And they didn't hand over some cool cash to your friendly neighborhood Anglo-Saxon male Whig on trial for snitching the Charmin; they gave it to a black female atheist Communist revolutionary.

Well, when that snippet of news hit the United Presbyterian hot line, the Scotts Turf Builder also hit the rotor lawn mower. Not a few folks were more than just a little miffed. But for the fact that we live in such a humane, enlightened age, there would have been demands for executions at sunrise and boilings in oil. As it was, there was sweeping enthusiasm amongst the ranks to fire most of the national staff and half the United Presbyterian pastors in the country, 99.99 percent of whom knew nothing of the transaction until they too felt the Turf Builder stinging their exposed epidermises.

That one minor incident is still having repercussions today, years after it happened. It was a major indiscretion over a minor incident, in my opinion. Nevertheless, that $10,000 grant probably has meant the loss of $100,000,000 to the United Presbyterian Church nationally, regionally, and locally. People voiced their opposition by withholding their funds, and some of them are still doing it. There is not a United Presbyterian parson who has been ordained more than six months who hasn't heard about Angela Davis from someone. If I ever meet her, I'd like to suggest to her that if religion is the opiate of the people, inadvertently she has done more than anyone else to break United Presbyterians of a bad habit.

About A.D. 67 a tentmaker-turned-apostle stood in a courtroom in Caesarea on the Mediterranean coast northwest of Jerusalem. He was the same apostle who said that governing authorities are there by divine behest, and you ought not try to overthrow them. At Caesarea, Paul was not trying to overthrow them, just to win them over, the "them" being a Roman governor and a Jewish king. Since that time, many Christians and churches have attempted in one way or another to influence politics and politicians and affairs of state and the course of nations.

There is only one way to avoid the problems that such actions invariably create every now and again, and that is to refrain from all political activity of any kind. It is to turn the church into a totally unstained, spotless bride, who is in the world but has absolutely no part of it.

One enormous danger looms up, however. "God alone is lord of the conscience." The conscience of one person or one church may dictate abstinence from all political and worldly activity, while the conscience of another person and another church may demand initiatives of a political and social nature. You can inform conscience and you can try to turn it in particular directions, but you can't negate it. If you try, you do so at your own peril.

So the church sets itself up for a perpetual war over its own nature. Shall it be the Spotless Bride of Christ, or shall it be the Arbiter of Society?

In terms of history, whenever the church has been virtually unstained from the world, it has done almost nothing to change the world. And when it has been politically so powerful that it actually became the arbiter of society, it was impossible to distinguish the church from the world around it, and its identity was lost.

Thus it is somewhere between the unworldly bride and the ecclesiastical-political juggernaut where the battle over the nature of the church is fought. But you may be sure that it is a battle, and you may be certain that it has been and is being and shall be fought.

Because the conflict has gone on for nineteen centuries, there seems to be little hope that we are about to end it and clear up the issue of church and state once and for all. All Christians and all churches must resolve the conflict as best they can in their own circumstances and for their own period in history, but no one is ever going to straighten it out for everyone for always.

It makes for a lovely, lively, lengthy debate.

Who Wins?

It has been the thesis of this short book that it is in the nature of the church to have a continuous internal battle over the nature of the church. Christians are people who should be deeply concerned about what the church is and what it does. But because there are so many different kinds of Christians, in terms of both personality and theological or denominational persuasion, it is impossible that there can be a universal uniformity in our understanding of the nature and purpose of the church.

I have tried to suggest a few examples of the kinds of issues that spark ecclesiastical warfare. No doubt you can supply many more.

Upon our initial inspection, ecclesiastical feuding, fussing, and fighting may seem to be not only counterproductive but also inimical to the very teachings of the man from Galilee who founded the church. Surely Jesus never intended us to carry on the way we do!

That thought produces a genuine dilemma. Just what did Christ intend for his church? Did he have any idea we would become such proficient infighters? Could he have foreseen the bitter warfare of Christians with other Christians?

The divine side of Jesus saw it all, because divinity sees everything. But the human side of Jesus could not have grasped the magnitude of the war within, because he could not have imagined the magnitude of the church. Nobody

living in Galilee in the first century could ever have imagined
the existence of a church building as immense as St. Peter's
in Rome or St. John the Divine in New York City, or even the
Church of the Annunciation in Nazareth. Jesus and his disciples would be absolutely thunderstruck by the size and
breadth of the Christian church in the twentieth century, by
the World Council of Churches and the many National Councils of Churches and the Vatican and the National Association
of Evangelicals and all the other organizations and alliances.
A billion Christians, a *billion* of them: no Jewish fishermen,
peasants, or tax collectors, or even a remarkable rabbi in
whom God dwelled in his fullness, could have foreseen what
was to become of the association of those thirteen men.

Nevertheless, though the church has grown into an incredibly complex organization, it has also developed an incredible strength and resiliency. A significant part of its strength
is its diversity. It offers so many avenues of discipleship that
virtually everyone can find a comfortable place somewhere
in its broad ranks.

There is no nation on earth where there are no Christians.
Even where governments have decreed that there shall be
none, there are Christians. Clandestine churches are meeting for prayer and worship every day of every week throughout the world, adhering to the promise of the Master,
"Where two or three are gathered in my name, there am I
in the midst of them" (Matt. 18:20).

Church people are a hardheaded crew. You can't keep
them down. Try to suppress them, and they will slip around
you. Try to ignore them, and they will surround you. The
world doesn't quite know what to make of these strange birds
who call themselves Christians. It never has figured us out.
It probably never will.

The world has problems with the church, and the church
says the feeling is mutual. But the church has far more trouble with the church than it has ever had with the world. We
just can't get our act together. The army of Christ is so busy
fighting one another that it can scarcely find time to do battle

with secularism, atheism, agnosticism, or communism. We have more than enough to keep us occupied with our own isms: Roman Catholicism, Methodism, Lutheranism, Anglicanism, Presbyterianism, Congregationalism. Toss in a couple of -als and an -ists, such as the Pentecostals, Evangelicals, and Baptists, and we have a delightfully volatile combination in the Mrs. Murphy's chowder which is the church of Jesus Christ.

The apostle Paul understood the nature of denominationalism long before there were any recognizable denominations. In I Cor. 11:18 and 19, he says, "When you assemble as a church, I hear that there are divisions among you; and I partly believe it, for there must be factions among you in order that those who are genuine among you may be recognized." Most Christians down through the centuries have not been bashful about asserting that they were themselves the genuine and official article, nor have they hesitated to declare that other people were unofficial, inauthentic second-rate copies of the real thing.

It would be a mistake to try to negate the harm that has resulted from the diversity of the church. More than that, it is impossible to negate it. Untold thousands upon thousands of people have been slaughtered like so many sacrificial lambs because of religious differences that have erupted periodically. The idea was this: if you disagree with your theological or ecclesiastical adversary, do him in. It's quick, it's painless (for you), and it gets results.

We should not think that this carnage is all pre-twentieth century, either. One only has to ponder the situation in Northern Ireland to realize that bloody differences still haunt the church of the Prince of Peace. I doubt whether the people of Ulster are more cruel than other people, but surely some of them are more inflexibly convinced that they are right than most of us are. The rigidity of both parties has led to the almost complete collapse of their way of life. Still the strife goes on.

No, there is no getting around the damage of the war

within the church. The casualty totals in misspent energy, misplaced zeal, misguided actions, and misused power are horrifying.

However, there is one saving grace. The church is not simply the church of Methodists, Presbyterians, and Roman Catholics, or Norwegians, Vietnamese, and Australians; it is the church of Jesus Christ. No matter how completely it may appear that human beings have destroyed ecclesiastical peace, unity, and purity, God manages to come through and save the day. He's like that, you know. He is *God.* And he won't leave himself without a witness.

The critics of the church invariably fail to remember the divine ace up the church's sleeve. They look at the church and they see people: muddled, soiled, sinful people. People are obviously the problem of the church. But they are not the solution. God is.

Why can't the critics get that straight? Why can't the critics within the church get it straight? Seeing people as the church's main problem takes no skill at all. It's like looking at a flat tire on a car and deducing with an unparalleled burst of brainpower: "The trouble with this car is that it has a flat tire. You can tell. See those other three tires? They're round. See this one? It's flat, at least on the one side."

Fantastic! Stupendous! Magnificent! Except for one thing: the problem is not a flat tire at all. It is instead that the tire has a hole in it someplace or that the valve is leaking. In any case, the tire is unable to repair and then reinflate itself. It needs assistance from outside if ever it is to return to its intended bulgy-cheeked roundness.

The church too has its problems overcome from outside. By ourselves we'll never succeed. We can make it only with God's help. And let us repeat: God will not leave himself without a witness.

Now that's not to suggest that God is delighted with every Christian who has come down the pike, or that he goes wild with joy at every harebrained idea concocted by every harebrained would-be disciple; not on your tintype, should you still have one lying around someplace.

Furthermore, I do not mean to imply that every conceivable stance that might be taken by or in a church is okay. Some of the positions we take are simply unacceptable, yea verily, outrageous, no matter how firmly we may believe in them. I am reminded, for example, of a medieval theologian whose name I happily have forgotten, who was trying to magnify the divine nature of Jesus by downplaying his human nature. In Jesus' conception, gestation, and birth, this gentleman asserted that "Jesus passed through Mary like water through a tube." Well, that is undiluted nonsense. I admire the fellow for perceiving divinity in the man from Nazareth, but he was a theological cyclops. Apparently he had no other eye to see the humanity of Christ at the same time.

No, some of the things that Christians say and do can never be accepted. Nevertheless, it is okay that God allows us to say and do anything and everything in the church. What we do may not be *right*, but it is *acceptable*, because God's truth abideth still. It is proper and necessary that we should debate what his truth is, and how it applies to us in our time and in our circumstances. And it is inevitable that we shall disagree over what is God's truth, and what the real questions are, and what the real answers are, and what we should do, and how we should do it.

In the end, it is all to the good. Our war is not a fight to the death, nor a fight for life, but a fight for *new* life. Truth must continually be reexamined and rediscovered. Hence the endless friendly and unfortunately not-so-friendly discussion, argument, and warfare.

The war within cannot kill the church, so long as our quarrels are lovers' quarrels. But dullness can certainly destroy us. If we fall into a complacent attitude, whereby we cease our debates over some of the questions raised here and the many other questions that arise by themselves, we shall cease being the living branches of Christ's vine.

Church battles are thus a sign of life and hope. Whenever the church is so tranquil that no voices are raised to protest or profess something or other, we have big troubles. Dullness brings deadness; disagreement brings life.

I remember being invited to the golden wedding anniversary party of a wonderful couple who were pillars of the church. They had oodles of friends, young and old, and everyone was as happy for them as they were for themselves. There was no doubt that they were and had always been in love.

They were great comedians, this pair. What Mr. Smith (a pseudonym) didn't think of, Mrs. Smith did. He was Abbott to her Costello, and she was Laurel to his Hardy.

At the party, one of those momentary lulls fell over most of the conversations. At that instant, someone happened to be speaking to Mr. Smith. "Well, George," she said, "I would imagine that anyone who managed to stay married fifty years must never have had any serious arguments."

"Never had arguments!" said Mr. Smith, typically overplaying his incredulity. "There was never a day when we didn't have one. And I lost every one of them. Here, I have the scars to prove it," said he, flipping off his coat, and loosening his tie. When he began to unbutton his shirt, his bride of fifty years stepped over beside him, gently laid her hand on his shoulder, kissed him, and announced that if he didn't start behaving himself she'd give him a scar he'd never forget. "Yes, dear," was his falsely sheepish reply, barely audible over the pleased chuckles of their friends.

Truth is often spoken in jest. My guess is that the Smiths did have their share of marital disagreements. But it did not detract from their marriage; it enhanced it. They had learned the secret of fair fighting, and they were the better for it.

Fighting that is not fair is bad fighting. Too much fighting is bad. This applies to the church as much as to marriage. But if the battle is productive, and is meant to edify the church rather than injure it, the results will prove to be most beneficial. This is part of the theme from William Walsham How's great hymn, "For All the Saints Who from Their Labors Rest."

Thou wast their Rock, their Fortress, and their Might;
Thou, Lord, their Captain in the well-fought fight;
Thou, in the darkness drear, their one true Light.
Alleluia! Alleluia!

O may Thy soldiers, faithful, true, and bold,
Fight as the saints who nobly fought of old,
And win with them the victor's crown of gold.
Alleluia! Alleluia!

And when the fight is fierce, the warfare long,
Steals on the ear the distant triumph song,
And hearts are brave again, and arms are strong.
Alleluia! Alleluia!

The church of Jesus Christ is breakable, but it is not fragile. It can withstand some pretty rude shocks. In fact, it needs a good shaking up every once in a while as a test for any cracks that may appear in its exterior walls. That way, little cracks can be discovered and can be repaired before they become big cracks.

The war within provides the shaking. Human nature causes Christians to disagree with one another, and to seek to win victories in the disagreements. But God, who created man in his own image, intends many of our disputes to occur. They are a reflection of the conflict he sometimes feels within himself over what he should do and what is the proper direction for his world and his church.

Here and there the church will get sidetracked or even derailed by its internecine battles, and that is unfortunate. Nevertheless, God is not ultimately concerned with here and there. Oh, *here and there* he is concerned about here and there, as he pours himself into the issues of the world, but *ultimately* he gives himself to eternity. And because his kingdom ultimately is eternal, and he is God, he is going to win.

The church is one of the agents of his victory. I am enough of an ecclesiophile to believe that it is his primary agent, so long as the church is seen as an extension of Christ in the world. The church is the body of Christ, the organism through which Jesus Christ becomes manifest in the world.

The most serious institution in human history is the church. But the church ought not to take itself too seriously. Otherwise it will suffer from that not-so-rare and generally fatal disease, indispensableitis. The *church* is indispensable, but the Roman Catholic and Southern Baptist and Presbyterian and Seventh-day Adventist and Nazarene churches are all dispensable. At one time each of them did not exist. At some future time each of them might not exist again, though I doubt that all of them shall pass. Some form of denominationalism is always necessary, lest the losers in the struggles within Christianity find themselves without a place to go. The best examples of denominations evolved because certain Christians had deep convictions which are within the broad limits of the one holy catholic apostolic church, but who didn't fit into the more constricted limits of other denominations within the holy catholic church. The worst examples of denominations evolved because certain Christians had an acute capacity for hatred, bigotry, and feelings of theological or ecclesiastical superiority.

I have a favorite metaphor for the church, and I like it so well because it comes from my favorite mentor in the church, Dr. Elam Davies, pastor of the Fourth Presbyterian Church in Chicago. The church, he says, is a creaky old ship that finds itself caught in a raging storm. You look at it as its prow plunges into the trough of a giant wave, and you think it cannot avoid going straight on down to the bottom. The crest of the onrushing wave smashes over its bow, and it appears as though it is finished. But then, hurling the spray from its groaning decks, the bow emerges again, bravely rising up to face the next wave.

We have taken a terrible buffeting in the history of the church, and we haven't seen the last of it. The war within is both necessary and costly, requiring continuous maintenance and restoration.

Thank God none of us is the captain of this ship. Were that so, we would be better off being thrown overboard, as Jonah was. Jesus Christ alone is captain, and God alone determines the course and the ports of call. Where we are headed we cannot know with absolute certainty, never having been there before.

But of this we can be certain: it is far preferable to ride out the storm in the creaking ship that is Christ's church than it is to build a boat of one's own, for in the words of the sailor's prayer, "The sea is so wide, and my barque is so small." Besides, it's a lot less lonely in the church than it is in your own boat.

The church will survive just about anything, short of mutiny. No matter what the world hurls against the church, or what the church hurls against itself, it has a fantastic record of survival. It isn't the crew that keeps the church afloat, though it has had some wonderful crewmen. It is the Captain. He knows his way around. And he will bring us safely to port.

•   •   •

Who wins the war within? The church wins. Christ wins. God wins.

And the world wins. The church exists for the sake of the world. It is Christ's instrument for the redemption of the world. I have it on good authority. "For God so loved the *world* that he gave his only Son, that whoever believes in him should not perish but have eternal life." (John 3:16.)

Church people aren't the only people who know the truth of those words. But they're the ones who should know it best.

Therefore they band together to plan the best strategy to get that Good News out to the world. In their planning they don't always agree. They often disagree. But they have a splendid time in their disagreements, if they aren't overly concerned about winning.

If God, Christ, the world, and the church win, then does it matter whether you or I win? It does to us, but ultimately it doesn't. However, in the temporality in which the church lives out its life, the battles continue.

Well, as they say in churches and in church councils from the Bering Strait to Tierra del Fuego and from New York west until you come all the way around to Paris, *c'est la guerre*. But also *c'est la vie*. That's war. That's life.

QUESTIONS FOR DISCUSSION

Introduction: The Nature of the Warfare

What characteristics in the original disciples made them so successful? What characteristics detracted from their success?

Why do we assume that the church cannot have both harmony and disagreement?

In your experience, are church controversies generally substantive, or are they generally emotional?

What kinds of issues cause the greatest controversies in the church? In your church?

What is the worst church "fight" you know about? How was it resolved?

Do Christians seem nicer and more reasonable and easier to work with than other people? If so, how? If not, why?

How can ecclesiastical battles be exhilarating? Edifying?

1. The Ideal Church vs. The Real Church

Can the church become ideal?

What examples of progress toward or regression from the ideal do you see in the church?

In what ways does Christ expect his followers to be different from other people? *Are* we different?

How are Christians similar to non-Christians?

If we really try to follow Christ, what kind of troubles are we bound to get into because of it?

In what ways do young people today seem more or less idealistic than the previous generation?

In what quarters of society, either within or outside the church, do you observe cynicism? How can we combat it?

2. HARD-CORE CHRISTIANITY *vs.* SOFT-CORE CHRISTIANITY

What are the hard-core denominations? The soft-core ones?

Is your congregation hard-core or soft-core?

What are the essentials of discipleship which Christ expects of all his followers, hard-core and soft-core?

What does it mean for someone "to take up his cross and follow" Christ?

What is your reaction to the statement, "God is easy on sinners, but hard on sin"?

Can one denomination or one congregation be both hard-core and soft-core at the same time? How? Or why not?

What should be the church's policy regarding baptisms, weddings, and funerals as it applies to members and non-members?

What minimal standards should be expected of church members in order to keep them on the congregational roll?

Does God feel ambivalence within himself over what he expects of us?

3. THE FORTRESS vs. THE FRONT LINE

Why did the church draw back into a defensive position during the Middle Ages?

From your understanding of history, what would you say were the primary motives behind the Crusades?

What do the majority of people in your congregation want your church to be, a fortress or a front line?

How is a congregation's mission and image of itself influenced by the location in which it finds itself?

In general, do you perceive the worldwide church as being in an offensive or a defensive position at the present time?

What position do you prefer for the church: (1) fortress, (2) front line, (3) neither, (4) other?

4. THE ARRIVED vs. THE ARRIVING

What does the question "Are you saved?" mean to you?

Are there any specific doctrines a person must believe in order to be saved, and if so, which ones?

Is your congregation composed primarily of born-again Christians who have arrived, or are your people in the Arriving category? How would outsiders answer this question?

Who determines who is Arrived or Arriving?

Is "arrival" an absolute or a relative (or an objective or a subjective) term?

5. GOD'S DEMOCRACY *vs.* GOD'S BUREAUCRACY

Why is there so much stratification in the church along economic, ethnic, and racial grounds? How can that stratification be broken down?

Why is the church sometimes insensitive to human need?

In your opinion, which system accomplishes things faster: a totally democratic system, a totally bureaucratic system, or something in between? (If between, *where* in between?)

In the Chicago Indian uprising mentioned herein, what do you think the church should have done?

What is the best political system for the church?

How can the church promote the best of both democracy and bureaucracy in its ranks?

6. THE SPOTLESS BRIDE *vs.* THE ARBITER OF SOCIETY

Is the world evil, good, or morally neutral?

Why is politics considered such a dirty business? Can politicians avoid being soiled by politics, especially elective politics?

Can Christians avoid being soiled by the world?

Is the church better or worse off when it cooperates with government?

Has the concept of the separation of church and state worked to the advantage or disadvantage of the church in our nation?

Should people who break the law on grounds of conscience suffer as strongly from the consequences of the law?

Under what circumstances might the church support revolutionaries?

Under what circumstances is the church most effective in helping to shape the course of secular affairs?

CONCLUSION: WHO WINS?

Is it natural for the church to have conflict over the nature of the church?

What kinds of conflicts might God support within his church? What kinds might he oppose?

Is it possible that someday there might be no church at all?

Are there any theological or ecclesiastical positions so outrageous that just to speak of them threatens the existence of the church? If so, what are they? If not, then why are we so fearful of controversy?

How does the church take itself too seriously?

In your discussions about this book, have you reached unanimity on everything discussed?

How do you feel about one another if you didn't reach unanimity?